BREAK FREE!

Understanding and Overcoming Disordered Fear

CHRISTOPHER WILGERS

WESTBOW·
PRESS
A DIVISION OF THOMAS NELSON
& ZONDERVAN

WestBow Press books may be ordered through booksellers or by contacting:
WestBow Press
A Division of Thomas Nelson & Zondervan
1663 Liberty Drive
Bloomington, IN 47403
www.westbowpress.com
1 (866) 928-1240

ISBN: 978-1-4908-2246-4 (sc)
ISBN: 978-1-4908-2245-7 (hc)
ISBN: 978-1-4908-2247-1 (e)
Library of Congress Control Number: 2014900902

Printed in the United States of America.

WestBow Press rev. date: 1/27/2014

To the two most influential women in my life. First, to my mother, who never stopped believing in me, praying for me, and encouraging me through every peak and valley of my life; her depth of heart and spirit is an inspiration to all who know her. And second, to my wife, Tammy, whose untiring, sacrificial, and unfaltering loyalty and commitment to everything good have provided me the strength and determination to write this book. I love you both!

Contents

Part Three
Thoughts and Studies

Introduction

I remember it clearly: June 9, 2012. It was a beautiful Saturday with light swirling winds. I suppose it was a pretty common spring day in the Rocky Mountains west of Fort Collins, Colorado. We had resided at this small mountain acreage for over ten years. It was tinder-dry that day, but I felt as safe as one could, given it was yet another high-threat fire season brought on by the ongoing drought. By now we had gotten rather used to the annual forest fire threat. I took confidence in the fact that I had thinned out at least one-third of our trees. We had very good *defensible space*, a term you become very accustomed to when you live in the mountains. Additionally, we were on a relatively flat area, which gave us added protection from fires that might flare up. And for an added bonus, we knew that the Lord had led us to this home a decade ago. The house and the trees were well anointed and prayed over. Ours was the model home in our area and the one that would survive a fire.

It was around noon, and my son, Luke, and I were getting ready to head into town to take in a local car show. It was Luke who pointed out the dark, funny-looking cloud just west of our home. Our border collie was acting a little restless, a little more hyper then he usually was. It wasn't long before the familiar smoke smell and feel began to invade the senses. We'd been through this before. The fire crews always got on these very fast to snuff them out. All the same, that anxious feeling in the gut, which seemed to precede the thoughts that would lead to fear, was there again.

I remember the first year I moved my family up to the mountain property. It was a dream, and God did indeed seem to miraculously open the door wide for it all to happen. Nevertheless, at that time, I remember feeling my decision to move my family up into the mountains was probably one of the bigger mistakes of my life. It was 2002, and that spring and summer made up one of the worst, driest seasons on record. I had no clue how much of a threat the fires were, and I slept very lightly those summer nights. After that first year, conditions got somewhat better, I learned some lessons, and the fear of fire, while always present, seemed manageable.

I decided that with this new little fire, a long way off and clearly moving in the opposite direction, I didn't need to get too alarmed. Nevertheless, we canceled our trip into town to keep an eye on things. I cannot accurately portray how this little smoke cloud began to evolve into the most ominous-looking thing I had ever seen. While we learned it was several miles away from us, it still looked like a fire-breathing monster looming just over the first hill. Huge black billows with bright-red fringes were quite observable to the naked eye. It was horrible-looking, and that fearful uneasiness was creeping deep within us. We began to prepare just in case we got the reverse-911 call that comes when and if it is time to get ready to evacuate. This had happened a couple of times before, and it had always turned into nothing. Even though the commotion amongst our mountain community began to intensify, I felt a peace knowing that God would take care of us and our property. The next few hours were very stressful. You rehearse in your mind what to do, what you will take, but when it comes down to it, you go a little brain-dead, and you end up packing odd things and leaving obvious things behind.

And then the call came. We were to evacuate. The winds had become crazy-hot and unruly. Still, it seemed the fire was moving away from us, and we thought the authorities were just being cautious and we would be back home in a day or two. We scrambled to load up what we could think of in my wife's Honda Pilot and in my truck and trailer. We had a little trouble getting our distressed dog, Obi, into the car, but once he was in we were off, praying as we left our home. I could see black and red skies growing larger in my rearview mirror. Little did we know, that would be the last time we would ever see our home, our beautiful green pine trees, and my cherished barn, which I had converted to a woodshop housing thirty-five years of accumulated tools. From my parents' home in Fort Collins, where we decided to evacuate to, we could see what looked like an Armageddon over the foothills for several days. Ashes were falling over the town like large snowflakes, even finding their way into cars. Those with respiratory issues were to stay indoors. The rancid smoke odor permeated even the inside of the home whenever a door was opened. The surrealism of the whole event was perhaps the most unsettling thing I have ever experienced. Fear was indeed ever lingering, as we knew many homes were being lost and we wouldn't be able to know for days if we had a home or not.

Exactly seven days after we evacuated, we learned that our home, my woodshop, and all the contents within were gone forever. They were completely consumed on June 10. The High Park Fire was the worst fire in Colorado history, with over 280 homes burned to the ground. The whys to God went on for days. After all the prayers of protection from so many, our beloved home and all our belongings had perished. I learned many things from this experience. I learned that God is good despite all that happens in this life. The greatest lesson, perhaps, was that the fear that I had lived with of actually losing our home and everything we owned was much greater than actually losing them. Fear must be understood and overcome.

This book has been in my heart and in my head for many years now. The thoughts and conclusions I am presenting here are intended to lead you, the reader, into deeper levels of introspection concerning this nagging force, which motivates us toward many destructive habits of the mind, which in turn leads to destructive behaviors as well. I understand that it is a hefty undertaking to address such an adversary as *fear*; nonetheless, I cannot escape years and years of accumulated conclusions from the realm of my Christian counseling practice that nearly all of our emotional, spiritual, and mental struggles are rooted in distorted, *disordered* fear. I now humbly present to you an effort that has been years in the making.

Part One
Understanding Fear

1

Fear: The Great Paradox

Fear is an all-pervasive problem of humankind, and it cohabitates with us with great tenacity. Life is ever changing, and new societal fears are ever emerging. The only certainty seems to be that we are a terribly fearful people, yet ironically a people who were never intended to live in such fear. Something is going terribly wrong here. It is not our heavenly Father's will or purpose for His children to live in such *disordered* fear.

As I have labored over two decades leading people toward psychological and spiritual healing, I have come to a conclusion: regardless of what symptoms and apparent issues are manifested, most of us seem to suffer from a common condition that I will call throughout this book, *disordered fear*. I have found it to be at the center of nearly every emotional/psychological struggle. It seems to dwell at the very core of the heart, or what we now call the *unconscious self*. People hold in the heart two seemingly contradictory forces, which are the two great motivators of humankind: *fear* and *love*. As a Christian therapist, I have sat hours in the company of people with wounded hearts, broken hearts, and hardened hearts. Every working day, I experience individuals and families who are suffering terribly. Many seem to live in despair and anguish continually. I see minds filled with lies their pasts have taught them, leading to immeasurable pain. And at the bottom of this, I find fear.

Many years ago I read M. Scott Peck's popular book *The Road*

Less Traveled.[1] I was struck by his simple opening sentence: "Life is difficult." In the early days of my career, it had always been my intention to reduce, or even eliminate, this "difficulty" in the lives of my counselees. I was naïve, but the intention was a good one. Today, I know that suffering is, and will always be, a part of our earthly existence. However, I also fully believe that if we can confront the core condition of being dreadfully afraid, we can then overcome our own inner divisions that lead to a host of neurotic symptoms and addictions, and undue suffering. We will then be able to live in the wonderful freedom (freedom from fear) that God intends for His children.

After doing an exhaustive search in Scripture for an enlightened understanding of this *disordered fear,* I found approximately five hundred occurrences of the word *fear,* or variations of it. I found that two clear themes were presented. One was always quite negative and alluded to a notion of terror, deep anxiety and unrest, and punishment. And the other form, which was positive, spoke more to an overwhelming reverential fear of God. It is quite fascinating how closely these two types of fear are related to each other in both the Greek and Hebrew texts. Over and over I came across the theme *fear not ... fear not ... fear not ...* And equally I found the repetitious *fear God ... fear God ... fear God ...* A conclusion that cannot be overlooked is that, paradoxically, we apparently were created to fear, and yet are also to be free from fear. In other words, our hearts are fashioned with a beautiful burden to love, worship, and fear, and intriguingly these three concepts are profoundly related to each other. The intent of this book is to explore the many facets of love and fear, and to humbly provide some helpful healing conclusions as to how we, the children of God, need to combat disordered fear in our lives.

All human motivation springs forth from love and/or fear. The potentially negative context can find us caught up in a relentless process whereby we end up becoming enslaved to that which we fear (e.g., poverty, illness, loneliness, insignificance, people, etc.). As a result, we can quite easily obsess about our desire and *love* for perhaps wealth, comfort, and material accumulation, or maybe our health and physical fitness, or perhaps prestige and status, or maybe even relationships. Where we may work hard to seek after these unique loves of ours, we inherently also fear the lack or absence of them.

The positive side of love and fear will seek after what we were created for (i.e., God; His kingdom and His righteousness). Scripture teaches us that we cannot serve God and mammon. We will love the one and hate the other.[2] And also that "where our treasures lie, there also are our hearts (i.e., what we love).[3] We are to love and tend to that which is of an eternal nature, not that which is temporal, which moth and rust can eat away.[4]

Love *and* fear will commingle and cohabitate. We must learn and understand the functional, holy side of love and fear as well as the disordered, destructive side, which leads to all sorts of neuroses and addictions. The question at hand is always to which side of love do we yield?

Moreover, we were all created to worship. It is in our spiritual DNA. We cannot, *not* worship. All human beings engage in this act. Unfortunately, all too often our worship is directed toward the temporal. These things, which usually have material form, never satisfy. They provide the unconscious with substance from which strongholds (things that have power over us) and addictions spring forth. Sometimes these strongholds have socially commendable forms such as avid physical fitness or vocational accomplishment and excellence. These things, put into a moderate balance, are not necessarily bad; it is only in their extremes, driven by disordered fear, that they can become a destructive form of worship.

Each time a new individual comes in to me for counseling, in the back of my mind I have the question, "What are the *addictions*, the things that are holding you back, and the strongholds that must be overcome?" *Addiction* is not a term we find directly in Scripture, but it is alluded to often. It can be defined as anything that has power over us. This could be either negative (that which is temporal) or positive (that which is eternal), but the point is that we all have some thing or things that have mastery over us, and that is precisely what we end up serving. That is what we, willingly or not, end up worshipping with our time, attention, and energy. Consequently, that is what we end up loving *and* fearing. And when that is anything other than God Himself, it becomes the *disordered fear* and stronghold that holds us captive and keeps us from enjoying the abundant life that Jesus came to bring us.[5]

The nature of a stronghold is that we are never satisfied. There can never be enough. I have yet to meet a financially wealthy man or woman (at least in the context of my counseling practice) who didn't strive for greater financial success. Nor have I ever seen an athlete satisfied with his or her latest achievement. We are always striving for the next obtainable, measurable symbol of our success. Once this symbol is obtained, disillusionment often follows, and we must then find the next thing or symbol to demonstrate our significance to others and to ourselves. The paradox is that when such things are pursued from the disordered fear motive rather than from the God/love motive, then neurosis in the form of anxiety, depression, anger, phobias, new addictions, restlessness, and even physical illness can often result.

Scripture teaches that we will and must fear, and the only suitable recipient is God alone. Through the fall of man, this God-ordained need has deviated toward self-serving fears: fear of people and their opinions, fear of failure, fear of poverty, fear of illness, fear of rejection, and the greatest fear of all, the fear of death itself. These fears are all a result of the fall of man. With this, all kinds of addictive strongholds have taken root in our hearts, our unconscious selves. But we must take heart; Jesus Himself told us that He came to leave us His peace.[6] I believe and have observed that if we will work to rectify this problem of *disordered fear* and go through the transformational process of heading back to the original intention—deep, awesome, and fearful intimacy with our creator God—we can experience the peace of soul, mind, and spirit that our Father has always wanted for His children.

2

The Five Fears

Before I address in more detail how disordered fears manifest themselves internally and externally in our lives, I would like to comment on, and validate, that there is a healthy type of fear (outside the obvious fear of God, which I articulated in chapter 1), which is rooted in the concept of reverence and respect for one's life. This type of fear is our comrade, and its purposes are self-preservation and survival. This fear is inherent in all healthy and rational people. With few exceptions, striving to remain alive and to thrive is at the core of every creature. One need not look any farther than nature to see that all living creatures—trees, plants, fish, and every sort of animal and insect alike—seek to live. Each seems to intuitively know that it is created to live and that, as our Creator has said upon viewing His creation, "It is good."[1] While the emotion of fear appears to be unique to humans and most mammals, the fight for life is evident in all living organisms.

It is not difficult to believe, therefore, that the Creator God Himself stamps this constructive motivation, which is reverence and love for life, into the psyche of every human soul. And it is this healthy fear that perpetuates our existence. For example, it is wise to fearfully flee from danger. We will want to withdraw from dangerous animals, dangerous people, starvation, disease, poverty, and natural disasters. The list goes on. This fear is healthy, and its basis and motivation are found in healthy love and reverence for one's life. Those who intentionally harm themselves by not fearing (respecting) danger have an unhealthy perspective on the beauty and goodness of life.

While *disordered fear* can take on innumerable forms, for the sake of clarity I have broken disordered fear into five primary categories:

1. The fear of things
2. The fear of people
3. The fear of failure and insignificance
4. The fear of the unknown/the fear of loss
5. The fear of suffering and death

I believe we can place each of our fears into one of these five categories. I have also ordered these five fears in accordance with the difficulty of the potential power and the strong hold they can have over us. The more objective the fear, such as in my first listed fear, *the fear of things*, the easier it is to identify, and therefore the easier it is to reverse. The more subjective the fear, such as *the fear of the unknown* and *the fear of suffering and death*, the more difficult it is to identify and reverse. However, the healing agent remains the same for each, and we, therefore, have an abundance of hope for overcoming our own personal fearful projections. I will now address each one of the five fears independently. It is not my intent to go into great detail regarding the common psychological interventions for dealing with such fears, but rather to lay these methods out as a backdrop for seeking the deep, healing touch of God, which is focused on in part 2.

3

First-Level Fear: The Fear of Things

By *the fear of things*, I mean the unhealthy projections we tend to place on particular things. This is quite different from the healthy fear of things that can indeed harm us in any number of ways. This category would include such objects as snakes and spiders, dogs and other animals, elevators and airplanes, heights and spaces, work and exertion, and other measurable, easily identifiable stimuli.

Perhaps you identify yourself with this category. We will also find that the five fears can easily overlap each other. In fact, we will tend to see that unresolved issues in the more objective categories of fear will almost always move progressively into the more subjective, abstruse, and immeasurable categories of fear.

While the fear of things can seem almost insurmountable and lead to fairly severe anxiety, such fears can be overcome by those who are willing to courageously face their identifiable tangible fears. I also want to add here that it is not always necessary to overcome all of our fears of things. Some such fears, irrational as they are, can be easily avoided. An example would be the fear of rats. This is not an uncommon fear, and, for the most part, rats can be avoided in life. Some would choose to simply stay away from areas or places where these rodents live.

Many might quote Scripture by saying that "God did not give us a spirit of fear..."[1] and that we should not have such strongholds. I contend that not all irrational fears need to be faced head-on unless an individual wants to. Not long ago I counseled a young man who had a fear of very large, unfamiliar dogs, as well as many other issues (fears) that were much more worthy of our attention. We reached a place in our therapy where he could actually see the reasonableness of his fear of large dogs. Acceptance of this idea was very therapeutic, and he was able to find a functional, sensible, and reverential fear of large dogs. He became able to walk by such animals that were on a leash or behind a fence with minimal anxiety. However, he had no desire whatever to learn to approach and pet one, let alone ever own one. This was practical. Some may say his healing was only partial, but he was quite happy with this outcome. Of course, unsurprisingly, this young man had had an unfortunate run-in with a large dog when he was young. We were able to identify why he was so afraid of big dogs and acknowledge that his fear was not entirely irrational, since large dogs can hurt people. However, he also learned that it was beneficial to not be overly controlled by his anxiety when the animals were not a threat. There are many such examples in which the acceptance and avoidance of a scary thing in one's life can be a completely valid and effective coping mechanism.

However, there are many more examples of the fear of things in which it is highly desirable to overcome the fear because it threatens the quality of one's life too much. An example would be a middle-aged woman I worked with who was dreadfully fearful of driving. This was severely limiting her quality of life and had become all-consuming. And while we must realize that many thousands of individuals have made the decision to not get a driver's license and to never drive, for most people this is far too limiting and unrealistic. With this kind of identifiable fear, there are some very effective therapeutic interventions that may be employed for those who are willing to suffer through the journey of healing. And since these *level-one* kinds of identifiable, objective fears are so prevalent, I will briefly outline some of the more effective interventions. In fact, some of these approaches can be very useful with the more subjective fears as well.

Identify the Origin of the Fear

While it is not popular today, with the current short-term-solution-focused demands (within the professional counseling setting) of insurance companies, as well as our current societal compulsions toward instant relief and gratification, I have found it to be extremely efficacious to explore with my counselees their childhood or early-life traumas, which may have led to the present disordered fear. We as humans have an impeccable need to understand the origin of our struggles and fears in order to begin to master them and heal from them. Exploring our pasts is not about needing to relive such traumas; it is about the need to share them with someone who cares and wants to help *carry their burdens,* as Scripture admonishes.[2] This type of healing love, brought about by a relationship with someone who cares in a compassionate way, can never be underestimated. It has never ceased to amaze me how much healing can occur by connecting soul to soul with another. If we can come alongside people in their fears and traumas, they (we) do not feel so much alone. This does not mean that counselors or helpers are to become enmeshed in the very same fear with which an individual struggles, but that the helper figuratively extends a hand into the person's life/ past in such a way that the sufferer does not feel alone. Investing time, effort, and energy into a person's past is the beginning of battling fear and trauma with God's love. We were never intended to journey alone in this life. Joining with another in personal battles, if only to walk alongside him or her, is the beginning of intimacy, which is the substance and bedrock needed to heal any fear.

For those who desire to embark on this journey, journaling can be extremely advantageous. We need only to go back as far as possible into our memories and start to record any events, themes, or impressions that at all have a traumatic feel. These can be quite subtle, such as being laughed at by peers or not being picked up on time by Mom or Dad after school when an individual was young. To many, these kinds of events do not carry very much weight into adulthood, but to other types of "sensitively natured" individuals, they can be of great significance in adult life. So for those who desire to begin contemplating earlier life experiences, it is best to be liberal with journaling and writing out events or memories that could be significant, rather than leave out important and helpful information for future work. After thorough reflection, certain insignificant entries can be eliminated before the hard work begins. Too many people, however, try to dismiss past events because dwelling on them seems silly or childish, when in reality they carry significance and do relate to current fears. So, again, it is better to err in the direction of listing too much past information than not enough. Let me stress, however, that this process is much more easily done with a skilled helper. In fact, journaling can possibly even be re-traumatizing if done without guidance and direction. For many people, it can be tough to deal with repressed emotions that may begin to erupt and fester back up into the conscious mind. Nevertheless, beginning to process through earlier life events can be very helpful in beginning to understand and overcome fear.

Progressive Relaxation

In combating our disordered fear of things, there is a very helpful behavioral technique called *progressive relaxation*. Briefly, this is a process by which we learn to relax and calm down our thoughts and our bodies. This is a type of mind and body meditation. The following simple description will give you an outline on how to practice this technique.

First, find a quiet place where you can be alone without being disturbed (this may be easier said than done). It is best to be sitting upright with both feet on the floor. Once this position has been established, close your eyes and begin to focus on your breathing. It is very helpful to get an image in your mind upon which you will focus. (I will address this practice in greater detail in the next technique I will describe, called *guided imagery*.) You then proceed to progressively relax each part of your body from the feet up. It is not my intent to go through all the sequential steps involved in this process. A therapist would be very helpful with this procedure, and there are also wonderful audio sources that walk a listener through this exercise to relax. This is a common behavioral therapeutic intervention and is effective at reducing the stress that contributes to fear and anxiety. However, this is not adequate in defeating the source of the fears in one's life. Nevertheless, it is a helpful technique to managing our anxieties. One can certainly learn more about this commonly used technique by searching online. The "Jesus Prayer," which will be discussed in detail in part 2, is often used in conjunction with progressive relaxation for Christians in order to reduce the physical and mental anxiety brought on by fearful thoughts.

Guided Imagery

This technique is often incorporated with progressive relaxation. Some Christians believe that this technique is worldly and not biblical. I have not found any scriptural prohibitions against such a practice. It is merely about closing one's eyes and visualizing something beautiful and peaceful. In more detail, once you are able to reach a relaxed, meditative state, you then guide yourself, in your imagination, to a certain comforting place or setting. You might be resting in a peaceful meadow or walking through the woods or sitting on the seashore. Oftentimes we will visually be guided to Jesus, through whom we can find perfect peace, since we are in the presence of perfect love. I realize that for many Christians, this all sounds too much like Eastern religions and philosophies. In reality, Western Christian spirituality has employed such techniques for centuries. Visions and dreams have always been a major part of Christian tradition. Guided imagery is not in any way a form of hypnosis. We are in total and complete control. For those who are open to this type of *visual contemplation*, deliverance from fear can most definitely be enhanced. For those who are not comfortable with such a method, it is best to stick with the more cognitive approaches to reducing fear.

Cognitive Strategies

Cognitive strategies are very powerful when fully embraced. This is the combating of the fearful thoughts. We identify the lies we have believed, and we confront them, challenge them, rebuke them, and replace them with the truth that sets us free.[3] Cognitive methods of fear reduction are scripturally validated over and over: Take every thought captive unto Christ[4] ... Be transformed by the renewal of your mind[5] ... As a man thinks in his heart, so he is[6] to name a few.

Here, we believe there is an absolute truth, and that absolute truth is none other than Christ Himself, who is that perfect love that (who) casts out fear.[7] We must identify and confront our misbeliefs and replace them with scriptural truth about our situations. All disordered fears are rooted in our misbeliefs, or put another way, in the lies we believe. Again, this process of identifying, challenging, confronting, and replacing long-held unconscious misbeliefs is most effective with good help, since it is so hard to be objective with oneself. Our own belief systems have often been deeply established and practiced for perhaps decades. They can be quite deep and unconscious. There is much to be said for cognitive interventions when it comes to our fears, and I will reference our need for changing our thoughts throughout this book.

Systematic Desensitization

This is a process whereby we take some fairly small incremental steps toward the object of fear. Most often, the person will first reach a state of *inner calm* through the use of progressive relaxation, most desirably with the Jesus Prayer, before engaging in these anxiety-promoting activities. These sequential steps may be (and almost always should be) done first with our guided imagery exercise; it can be highly effective to take a person through the challenging steps first with this exercise. Again, one must first have reached a certain state of relaxation before the challenging steps are introduced and visualized. In our *active imagination*, a term coined by the deceased famous Swiss psychiatrist C. G. Jung, we mentally watch ourselves go through the steps one by one. A great deal of anxiety can be produced here, but if we can stick with the exercise, we will begin to desensitize ourselves to the disordered tangible fear with which we struggle. Once success is met with the visual exercises, it is time to proceed with the actual. Let's use the case study of the woman I discussed previously, who was terrified to drive. Here we, together, would come up with a list of steps and challenges, which would knowingly result in anxiety. The list would proceed from least threatening to the most threatening. It might look like this:

1. With a supporting friend, sit in your car in the driveway for one minute.
2. With a supporting friend, sit in your car in the driveway for twenty minutes.
3. Sit in your car alone. Work up incrementally to twenty minutes.
4. Sit in your car alone and start it. Let it run for five minutes.
5. With your friend, drive the car down the block and back.
6. Drive your car down the block and back by yourself.
7. With your friend, drive your car in very mild traffic for a few minutes.
8. By yourself, drive your car in very mild traffic.
9. With your friend, drive in increasingly busy traffic.
10. By yourself, drive in increasingly busy traffic.

The goal is to come up with steps that are challenging but not overwhelming. If the steps are too difficult, the individual will pull away with greater fear and frustration. If there are no challenges, or they are too minimal, gains will not be made and the status quo will be maintained. Once a person is able to master the step being worked on—progressing to a point of performing the action with a manageable level of anxiety—he or she is then ready to proceed to the next step. Many small steps may be involved in such a process, and some trial and error is to be expected. It will most likely feel like an individual takes two steps forward and one step back. It is paramount that an individual work through these steps with somebody who is patient, caring, and skilled.

I remember well a very negative experience I had with this when I was a very young man in my early college days. I was terribly shy and fearful of girls. But at the same time I longed for a relationship and to be married one day. I didn't know much about psychotherapy at that time of my life, but a psychologist who had an office in the church I was attending was recommended to me. I made an appointment. The counselor seemed friendly enough as I shared my fears with him. I told him about a girl in one of my classes whom I was attracted to. He proceeded that first session to take me through a guided imagery exercise in which I was to approach this girl and ask her out. He politely, yet forcefully, with my eyes closed, pushed me through this step-by-step. This process absolutely terrified and traumatized me. I was nowhere near ready to do that, and consequently, my fear was increased, not decreased. I did not have a trusting relationship with this therapist before this procedure was applied to my situation. It failed and backfired. I must admit that, when I became a therapist many years later, I threw out the baby with the bathwater by refusing to use this technique on anybody due to my own trauma with it. Later, I was able to see the value of the exercise but approached it much more gently and only after first establishing a trusting relationship with those I was counseling. Sensitivity, patience, understanding, and empathy are paramount in approaching and confronting the fears of others. Many well-meaning friends, including Christians, can be brutally insensitive when they are trying to help someone get past their fears. We need to use the same patience and gentleness with ourselves as well, as quite often we can be very scornful toward our own weaknesses and fears.

In this chapter I have set out to describe what I call first-level fear, or the fear of things tangible. I have briefly described a few common therapeutic techniques that are used to help manage and work through such common fears and anxieties. These are the fears and phobias that frequently seem to plague many people in our fast-paced, high-tech, high-production society. Although the mental and behavioral techniques I presented are very good and should be implemented and practiced with all those struggling with these disordered fears, I believe that deep and permanent healing takes place at the core of the heart of the individual. More on this will be uncovered as we proceed.

4

Second-Level Fear: The Fear of People

The *fear of people* (or perhaps more appropriately, the fear of the opinions of people) is an enormous problem today, and its significance is largely overlooked. It is a deeper-level fear because it is harder to understand. It is more vague and paradoxical. We are instructed by our Lord to love each other as ourselves.[1] But as I stated earlier, we tend to worship and serve what we love. This idea is all too apparent when it comes to others. Very often, from the time we are young, we learn to be afraid of others. People know how to wound, sometimes intentionally and sometimes unintentionally. The words of others have far more impact over the years than do fists. Most of us, it seems, are conditioned to be afraid of others. Remember how closely related fear and love are? We were created to love, and we were created to fear. We have learned to project this onto others in a profound way—perhaps in a way that God never intended.

One of the most common expressions I hear in counseling is, "I am a people pleaser." This statement is extremely revealing in regard to what many of us serve in life, and what it is that can have mastery over our lives. In and of itself, there is no real problem with wanting to please and contribute to other people's happiness. The problem arises when our identity becomes rooted in our need to please others. For if this is the case, as it is with many of us, we will fail often. This will affect our ability to love ourselves appropriately, and we will indeed end up loving our neighbors as ourselves—and that is skeptically, inadequately, and fearfully. Before we go into much detail regarding the fear (and love) of others, I would like to address loving oneself.

Loving and nurturing oneself gets very bad press in a large segment of Christianity. Once again we are dealing with the paradox. The wrong kind of love—the self-seeking, greedy, narcissistic kind—of course is destructive and will always lead to fear. But we must acknowledge that Jesus' teachings make an assumption that the sane person does indeed care for and love himself or herself. In fact, it is a prerequisite, I believe, for loving others appropriately. The kind of love that is appropriate regards nurturance, time, attention, and discipline. It is this same type of love that the healthy person will naturally apply to his or her own life.

But, of course, everything that God intended for good in us can go awry with the distortion of our Enemy working in collaboration with the world and with our flesh. In other words, the equation looks like this: the Devil + the world + the flesh = fear. I once heard a very appropriate definition for the acronym FEAR: false evidence appearing real. And this is exactly the case and is our focus of warfare.

The distortion of this fear of people has turned into a tragic reality that used to be known as *vainglory*. We don't hear much about that anymore. In simple terms, vainglory means that from a root of vanity, we seek and value other people's opinions of us above God's. We therefore strive to find approval, attention, and significance in the eyes and opinions of fallible humans. Needless to say, this is a problem that we must begin to turn around. Almost always this type of fear is camouflaged with symptoms that betray the actual problem of fear. Let's now take a closer look at the manifestations and effects of the disordered fear of people.

Anger

While anger cannot, by any means, always be related to disordered fear, unresolved anger almost always is. Scripture states that it is okay to "be angry *but do not sin*."[2] Anger actually is a healthy emotion and one that even comes from the very image of God. It is not hard to find the expressed anger of God throughout the Bible (which if discerned correctly can always be seen as the shadow of the light of the love of God). Anger serves a purpose. It is nearly always a call to action of some sort. And the action must always involve love in some way—perhaps even a healthy love (respect) for oneself. Remember, as the Word of God Himself connotes, "Perfect love casts out fear."[3] And this type of *disordered* anger of which I speak is a symptom of that fear.

Whenever anger is an ongoing problem for a person, the fear of people must be seriously considered as a root condition. It is a very valuable exercise, with the help of another, to make a list of people who have harmed you in your life. The purpose is not to dredge up old wounds, but to reflect on and examine whether or not resentment and bitterness, which are like an emotional cancer, are present. This certainly can cause a generalized fear of people.

Emotional wounds often have their origin in childhood. Most children, being immature and naïve, will believe that wounds inflicted upon them by others, are a result of their own failure and inadequacy. Over time, in order to not get hurt any further, an emotionally injured person will likely build up a resistance to others in order not to get re-wounded. This wall, or defense mechanism, is most often constructed through the unconscious use of anger. This anger will inevitably lead to resentment. Resentment, as Scripture teaches, leads to a root of bitterness.[4] And bitterness will lead to hatred, which almost no one will admit. Such resentment or hatred actually serves a purpose, however. One cannot get re-wounded if one hates. This is a self-preserving coping mechanism that is, in all honesty, effective … if the goal is to not get re-wounded or re-traumatized. It does work, in the short run. The problem, however, is that harboring hatred circumvents the very thing we were all created for: to love completely and to be completely loved.

Another interesting twist can happen here, which is at the other end of the spectrum: the need to make certain that we offend nobody, ever. We so desperately feel our need to be loved, usually to compensate for our perceived lack of love, that we overshoot the mark and do only those things that will lead to positive affirmation from others. We try to please everyone.

When I ask those whom I counsel if they have forgiven their offenders (which thereby frees them to live at peace with themselves), many say, "I think so." The following are four ways to tell if we have forgiven someone:

1. When you think of the one who hurt you, does it still bring up negative, painful emotion?
2. Do you still ruminate over the offense committed against you?
3. Is there any unidentified anger spilling over into other relationships?
4. Do you justify the actions of the offender because "he or she couldn't help it; he or she was treated abusively also"?

If any of these are present, it is worth taking a deeper look into the matter to see if the process of forgiveness and healing is complete, and we need to look closely at fear of people being an underlying issue.

Hatred

In addition to what I said above, hatred as another possible symptom of the fear of people should be noted on its own. Hatred is the obvious conclusion of the type of anger that leads to resentment, and then bitterness. Resentment is the central point here. It has been said that resentment is like taking poison and waiting for the other person to die. It is self-perpetuating and cyclical. That is, the more one hates another, the more fear there is for that person, and, consequently, the more there is a need to hate in order to protect oneself from future harm. I believe it is fair to say, then, that whenever hatred is present, some form of fear is also present. Unless this issue is addressed and worked through in a safe environment, the fear and suspicion of people will increase and interfere tremendously with one's quality of life. Anger and hatred will often lead to depression as well.

Avoidance

This is perhaps the most obvious manifestation of the fear of people. Certain personality types seem to be much more prone to this behavior than other types. Specifically, those who draw energy intrinsically (introverts) are more apt to avoid people. And in defense of them, it is often necessary for their well-being to do so. However, it is also easy for people of this personality type to develop an unhealthy, excessively used coping mechanism of avoidance and withdrawal. This can then lean too far in the direction of isolation, which can then cultivate into the disordered fear of people. This fear must be addressed by finding a balance that supports the heavy need for solitude and meditative practices, along with the recognition that none of us was created as an island unto oneself. It will be important to learn that for the sake of healthy living and in order to live out the mandate to love God, *and each other,* we do indeed need others. Having said this, however, I do believe it is possible that a very few do have the call upon their lives for a great deal of solitude and separateness with God in a type of setting where interaction with others is fairly minimal. Nevertheless, I believe that such a call, which I realize is controversial in varying Christian beliefs, is extremely rare, and for many it actually becomes a medium by which they are able to avoid intimacy due to a fear of people.

A prominent motivation for avoidance regards those who have been hurt, usually repeatedly, by one or more persons. We must also observe, however, that most people have been hurt by others, but not all use the coping mechanism of avoidance to excess. Again, the more *predisposed* personality types are apt to set up defenses of avoidance to deal with their fear of others. This is often the case because the inner pain experienced and stored up within these types of personalities is usually much greater than with those of a more exterior, resilient nature. I have also observed something of a paradox in my dealings with those who seem to carry quite a bit of fear and anxiety: those who suffer in this way are often deeply spiritual people of faith. And contrarily, I have seen that numerous individuals who have almost no religious leaning, interest, or spiritual faith at all seem to be relatively free from fear and anxiety. What a conundrum this appears to be. It does not make sense at face value. We would hope to think that those of faith would be free from disordered fear, but it is not always the case. I used to be baffled that Scripture says it is *perfect love* that casts out fear. Common sense told me it should be *perfect faith* that casts out fear; but Scripture does not say that. Nevertheless, while I believe that true faith is utterly paramount to get free from fear, and "the truth will set you free,"[5] it has layers to it. Finding this love-imbued form of faith that sets us free involves a very personal journey through our own emotional wildernesses. I will address this idea in much greater detail in part 2 of this book. For now, my point is that personality type does make a large difference when one looks at certain types of fear. Again, those who are more contemplative, sensitive, and introverted by nature can (but do not always) have greater tendencies toward using avoidance strategies that can build and reinforce a fear motive. I would like to add to this, however, that these types are also among many great and gifted saints of God.

Insecurity

It is probably fair to say that all fear is rooted in insecurity of some type or another. But I have found that insecurity is most indicative of the fear of others. We have learned and have been programmed to believe that what others think of us is, in fact, reality. If we think on this much at all, it is not difficult to understand how insecure this would make us. We are all born with a certain need for security and belongingness. The significant question here is "from where do we derive that security?" If it is from possessions, these will be our gods and we will fearfully serve, bow down to, and be owned by these perishable gods. If it is our youth and health that give us security, these are what will fearfully consume us. (See chapter 7, on the fear of suffering and death, for more on this.) But if we tend to seek out our security through the recognition, approval, and praise of others, this category fits very well. It will then be other people whom we will serve, dread, and fear. For of all of the insecurities just mentioned, seeking the validation and admiration of others will be perhaps the least likely to ever succeed in giving us any significant satisfaction, let alone providing us with security. This is primarily because the approval of others is horribly flawed, in that the thoughts and opinions of many people are very often based upon the twisted whims of the entertainment-obsessed culture of these times. So if we fall into this trap (which I believe many of us do) of seeking our security and significance through the attention, approval, and praise of others, we will certainly live in a great deal of distress and insecurity.

Self-Esteem

Very closely linked to the issues of insecurity we will often find those who declare that they have low self-esteem. This is a surefire indication that these individuals struggle with the fear of people. As a therapist, my feeling and belief has always been that it is often problematic when the word *self* is followed by a hyphen and another word, indicating *self* as central. I also realize, however, that in our culture the word *self-esteem* is used daily by people without much attention being given to it. As I stated earlier, we are certainly to love ourselves in the right way, so if that is what is meant by a good self-esteem, I am all for it! Christian teachings vary considerably as to whether we are to have high self-esteem or not. On one end of the spectrum we find teachings that say it is self-focused, sinful, and idolatrous to have a high self-esteem, and at the other end we are taught that we are sons and daughters of God Himself and should indeed think very highly of ourselves. As with everything, I think it is dangerous to live at either extreme. However, when individuals acknowledge that they have *low* self-esteem, it will almost always be a description of how they see themselves through the eyes of other people. That is like looking into a cloudy mirror. We tend to see ourselves as we perceive others to see us. The problem is that these mirrors are very faulty and very often lie to us.

There is one sure way to heal this common quandary with self-esteem: change the first word from *self-* to *Christ-*, and we will now be on the way to deep healing. The question should become "How is our Christ-esteem?" In other words, our goal is to see ourselves as Christ does, through His eyes. In fact, this is the answer to everything! This is the truth that sets us free. The point is that this, then, takes our eyes off other's opinions of us and back onto God's, thereby shifting our fear of people to the intended *fear of God*. Ironically, we will find that most often God's heart toward us is quite different and vastly more loving than those of others, or even our own.

So just what is God's perspective on us? I find it most helpful to ask how we see our own young children. And although our love for our own children does not compare with the love that God has for us, it provides a wonderful analogy. I love my kids beyond comprehension. I would do anything for them that would help them. They are mine and I am theirs, meaning I will always be their father and they my children. We belong to each other as God appointed it and wills it. And they are needy. Among many other things, they need help tying their shoes and dressing themselves in the morning. Do they mind my helping them with such things? Not in the slightest. They want help and ask for it. And I readily give it. And on the other end of the spectrum, I see them as becoming more and more capable. They are smart and able to learn. They are beautiful and talented, and I relish the opportunity to see them excel and succeed. I think I have made my point. I believe that Christ sees us very similarly. We are, every one of us, extremely needy (we cannot even breathe without God), yet we are also quite capable, gifted, and beautiful to our Abba. We need to see ourselves as such. It will keep us humble and keep us from becoming proud and conceited (with overly inflated self-esteem), and it will also keep us from feeling horrible about ourselves (low self-esteem). I am aware that this is easier said than done, but I just want to point out that this is our work. It is our goal.

And this concludes my thoughts on the power that the fear of people can have over us, along with ideas on some identifying issues. We must understand that the gripping disordered fear we have of people must be rectified and shifted to our heavenly Father. He is the only one who can possibly be the recipient of an appropriate, *ordered* fear. In Him all things hold together.[6]

5

Third-Level Fear:
The Fear of Failure

In my counseling practice, *the fear of failure* is cited as an underlying issue more than any other fear. I have also observed that when counselees were asked to define what this meant to them personally, many would struggle to come up with much substance. Usually, when we elaborate on a definition, we find that the fear is primarily related to what the world or culture defines as failure. This then would indicate that the primary underlying fear is once again the fear of people. Nevertheless, since it is so often brought up, let's look closer at the so-called fear of failure.

Failure is actually a completely subjective idea. Certainly we have created a system in our society that attempts to classify one's performance as being a success or a failure. Our school grading system, for instance, is probably the most obvious, with letter grades being attached to measured performance. Perhaps this is a primary reason why we have come to attach our self-worth to measurable criteria such as a grade, an income level, a certificate or degree, observable material possessions such as a home or car, or even perceived physical attractiveness. I suppose it would be hard to live life without some sort of scoring system; nevertheless, it has done immeasurable harm to those who don't come out at the top of this scale (which of course is the majority of us). This has all led to a setup for "failure" for countless scores of people.

Given this phenomenon, it is no wonder that so many people indicate they are immobilized under the fearful burden of failure. We also find closely related to this fear or concept the ideal of perfectionism, which is another societal measure of success. The irony to this notion, however, is that one fails constantly when one lives under the impossible weight of perfectionism, since perfection is unobtainable—at least in any sustainable way.

When I discuss with my counselees the reasons for their fear of failure, they often share a laundry list of apparent failures, mostly from childhood. Most of these "failures" were the perception of not living up to a measurable standard of performance; that is, academic, athletic, or even physical beauty. When such "failures" are closely examined, one discovers that all are the result of not living up to societal standards. Such protocols are apparently defined by those who seem to possess the power and authority to prescribe the norms by which we stand or fall, the norms by which we measure ourselves, or more dangerously, by which we measure others.

Consequently, I suggest that the fear of failure is actually the fear of not living up to the standards that have been imposed upon us by those who set the *modus operandi* of success and failure. The real problem, then, is not so much that others (popular society) set such standards of success or failure, but that we believe these standards to be true. We accept such standards and then cower in the shadows of not meeting or living up to them, and hence the fear that keeps us from living abundantly and joyfully takes on a life of its own.

To conquer the fear of failure, we must set out on the arduous task of going deeply into our paradigm of beliefs about ourselves (i.e., that we are terribly inadequate) and then into our deeply rooted beliefs about what is, in actuality, success and failure. The work that lies before us then is to tear into these faulty constructs and replace them with the truth of God's Word. What does *He* say about adequacy and competency, beauty and worthiness, success or failure? What does *He* say about what is truth? We must learn and strive to love and embrace this truth with all our mind, heart, soul, and strength. Then—and only then—do we allow the truth (Jesus) to set us free from the bondage of living (or failing) under human-contrived standards of success. I cannot stress strongly enough the binding, fearful, and crushing impact that believing and living under spurious law (societal norms of measuring a man's or woman's worth) will have on a person. And, likewise, the freedom experienced by those who have learned to reject such man-made laws of behavior and measurement, for the truth, have been nothing less than miraculous. It can actually be quite simple with the help of God. I have seen individuals who experienced abundant freedom by simply changing their belief of needing/seeking to be *perfect*, which inevitably set them up for repeated failure, to the seeking of *excellence*, which is quite attainable when correctly defined. Correct and true definitions are of the utmost importance in getting free from our disordered fears. In fact, we will find that changing our definitions in life is not only a key component to being healed from our fears of failure, but also a basis for all healing journeys, no matter what the stronghold may be.

Since the fear of failure is, in essence, an offshoot of the fear of people, I will not repeat information already discussed in the previous chapter, but I would like to conclude with this reflection: I believe we would all do well to limit our exposure to electronic media entertainment. We are inundated with hypnotic messages of what we need, or need to be, to be successful and happy. Advertising is psychologically designed (and proven) to very effectively program us into believing whatever those in power wish us to believe. It is primarily through such avenues that we learn to feel terribly inadequate about ourselves. It is based almost completely on a hierarchical establishment. If we are not possessing or living the life that "successful" people live, we are failing. This is powerful psychology, and it is very, very effective. It can almost emotionally destroy many people who consciously or subconsciously strive to live toward the top of the hierarchy of "success" as defined by our current consumer-targeted media. We will inevitably, every one of us, fail to reach these spurious media-driven, money-driven "ideals." To want and pursue such things will only succeed in keeping us wanting more—be it material possessions, status and image, physical beauty, or academic and career superiority. Keep in mind the wisdom of King David: The Lord is my Shepherd and I shall not be in want ...[1] To live in *want* of these artificial things is not a burden our Lord wants us to carry—and what a burden it is! There is simply no end to this anxious need to be "successful." And if such "success" be true, let us embrace societal failure in order to be set free from such a heavy burden, for we must never forget what our Lord says: "My yoke is easy and my burden is light."[2]

6

Fourth-Level Fear:
The Fear of the Unknown/
The Fear of Loss

The *unknown* can be an extremely troublesome and fearful concept for human beings. Many of us struggle exceedingly with not knowing what is coming or what is going to happen to us, or what we could potentially lose. The unknown can cause the strongest and the bravest among us to suddenly and without warning feel substantial trepidation. And this is what the fourth level of fear is all about—the fear of losing what we believe is essential in life for our happiness, security, and well-being. This *fear of the unknown* can be difficult to overcome because so much of the time we have no control over making known that which is unknown. However, there are also times when we could achieve this task but often don't or won't for fear of what we might find out.

It is here that a well-developed, mature faith in God, in His Word, and in what He is about becomes mandatory. Even though, as was suggested earlier, certain God-given temperaments do have a greater tendency toward fear-ridden difficulties than other differing temperaments, it is the absolute and unequivocal truth that those who have journeyed deeply and consistently with the Lord will be much better equipped to handle the perils of the unknown.

It is important and vital to know that our society has been

enamored with the possibility of *knowing* the future through all kinds of marginal means that are outside God's will, and are consequently prohibited by Scripture. These include fortune-telling, occultism, astrology, Ouija boards, transcendental meditation, Tarot cards, sorcery, witchcraft, and parapsychology, to name a few of the more common. These so-called future-predicting mediums generate billions of dollars of revenue annually. Unfortunately, even many self-professed Christians fall into these desperate attempts to know what the future holds. We apparently have a tremendous need to know what is to come.

There are times when God will ordain us to glimpse the future through the gift of knowledge, wisdom, or prophecy.[1] These gifts can certainly lead us into deeper understanding of future events; however, I find that more times than not, we are told to "Be still, and know that I am God"[2] and to rest in *His* knowing and *His* care.

It seems the primary struggles with the unknown almost always involve the threatened loss of one or more of the following: one's own health/life; a loved one's health/life; financial security; vocational security; dignity and respect; comfort; possessions; love; freedom; and control of oneself. While there are more fearful unknowns, most would fit into one of these categories. These are all things we might fear losing. In other words, this then is what we fear could become real: our own illness, suffering, and death; the illness, suffering, or death of a loved one; monetary insecurity leading to loss of material possessions; unemployment or miserable employment; appearing foolish; poverty; loneliness; being under the control of another; and the loss of mental faculties. I have witnessed all of these "potential" losses being dreadfully feared by many whom I have counseled over the years.

It is also of significance to know, however—at least in my clinical observations—that well over 90 percent of our fears of the unknown never come to pass. But as was stated earlier, the enemy we must battle is not the potential loss in our life, which I will talk more about in the fifth-level fear, but the fear itself. The disordered fear is the point of battle, not the object of the fear. It is never the object (health, wealth, prosperity, etc.) of loss that is the primary issue; that fearful spotlight is the enemy's ploy. If we are focused and obsessed with the object of the fear, we are being deceived, our passions are being misdirected, and we move into various disabling strongholds. The most common form is the addictive habit of worry, which will lead to obsession when not directed and curtailed in the proactive form that I call *godly concern*, or "healthy concern."

I believe the difference between *worry* and *concern* is the key and the answer here. Both are projections regarding the future and deal with the unknown. Worry is directionless and fruitless, with nowhere to go, and it leads to the attack upon our spiritual and emotional stability. Worry absolutely steals from us what is most important in life: peace of heart and peace of mind. Healthy *concern* always points us forward. It always proactively seeks what we need to do. It seeks wisdom. Worry is destructive. Healthy concern is constructive. Many would never consider worry to be addictive, but as defined earlier, anything that has a power over us can be considered addiction. I have never seen anything as addictive as worry. The more out of control our life feels, the more we worry, and the more we worry, the more our life feels out of control. Concern, on the other hand, looks upward. Worry is an unhealthy downward spiral back into the cyclical equation that produces fear: the flesh, the Devil (the author of the lie), and this world. Worry always anticipates the worst of the unknown. Concern can be, and should always be, grounded in hope, which of course is about casting our eyes on God Himself. Worry has no direction or hope. This is the stronghold. Worry can seem to have a life of its own and slowly consumes the psyche. The good news is that worry can be transformed to the healthier outlook of concern, which directs us out and up, as Jesus was constantly doing in the Gospels.

There is an irony concerning this fear of the unknown, and that is the avoidance tactic used by many of us to keep what is unknown, unknown. Out of fear of what might be discovered, we avoid the inevitable and remain locked into a state of immobilizing fear. While there is plenty of information that is not possible to know concerning our future, there is also a very large amount of information that is accessible. The most common form of avoidance I have seen involves medical problems. I have counseled many people who have suffered with unknown pain who have never gone in to a physician to check it out. The only real reason for this is the fear that something is *really* wrong. I have also worked with a number of individuals who will not confront a boss, friend, spouse, boyfriend, or girlfriend concerning "hunches or speculations"—imagined or not—that they fear could lead to potential job loss, a painful conflict or breakup, or something worse.

I recall a man I counseled with who was engaged to a woman who seemed to be exhibiting strange behaviors concerning a number of issues. The young man was so fearful of the relationship ending, due to his fear of uncovering the unknown, that he was not able or willing to confront his fiancée. Another counselee was a woman who was dreadfully fearful of what her husband might do when he found out she had racked up credit card debt. And although she seemed quite certain he would not become hostile, she wasn't willing to disclose her secret to her husband for fear of the unknown. So she ironically kept herself locked into this dark, awful fear of the unknown. And this fear owned her. She became a slave to it. This went on for months until she was finally able to muster the courage to confront this fear. When she did, the outcome was not nearly as horrendous as she had anticipated.

There are many such examples I could give. A great deal of work I have done with those locked into various fears has been to bring into the light that which is in the darkness so people can begin to heal. Those undefined fears we lock away in the dark are a continual stronghold for the Enemy of our souls. We must expose those things that we can and not hide in our fear. Like an addiction, the perceived fear will have mastery over us, and the fear will intensify and be compounded. I reemphasize that in the vast majority of cases, the outcomes that we fear never come to pass; but in those cases when the job termination is announced, the feared affair is true, the breakup happens, etc., the truth will lead us to eventual freedom, and healing steps will always proceed.

To summarize the fear of the unknown, we must be aware that it is always the *fear* that is the problem, not the *unknown*. There is absolutely nothing that God will not see us through—even the pending loss of life itself, which is the next and final (and most troublesome) level of fear I want to address: the fear of suffering and death.

7

Fifth-Level Fear:
The Fear of Suffering and Death

The fear of suffering and death (our own, or often worse, that of our loved ones) is the ultimate form of the fear of the unknown/ the fear of loss. It is the beginning and end of all fears. It is no coincidence that Christ said He came to abolish death, indeed, our very fear of death.[1] So if, through His infinite love, Christ gained victory over death through His own suffering and death, why do so many Christians *not* seem to be victorious over this fear? I think there are several reasons for this.

First, if we are honest with ourselves, we must admit that we struggle to live in such faith. Many of us have great difficulty believing what God says to be true is actually true for us. Do we really believe that God is in control of all things? And do we really believe that God loves us? If we truly believe what God says is true, we have absolutely nothing to ever fear—nothing at all! (Of course, I am not talking about the healthy reverential fear of those things that can truly harm our well-being as I addressed earlier, but of the disordered fear that this book is addressing.)

Jesus said that we cannot even fathom the wonders that God has prepared for us in the life to come—eternal life.[2] If we are to be completely accurate, we must realize that we are already in eternal life—even here on earth—because Jesus conquered death on the cross. It's been done. However, we do not live as though death has been conquered. In other words, we do not live by faith. The truth will set you free. But if we do not believe what is true, there is no freedom, but only fear. The truth is that fear is our enemy. Fear is produced when the unholy trinitarian union—the Devil, the world, and our flesh—work together against truth. In order to live in fear, we must cooperate with these three by believing the lies. Lies always lead to bondage, and bondage always leads to fear.

We as Christians should keep no company with the fear of bodily death. St. Paul even acknowledged it as gain.[3] It is—should be—our ultimate quest to enter the place/state where there are no more tears,[4] where we will be freed from these troublesome tents.[5] By faith we believe that what is to come is wonderful, glorious, beyond our wildest imagination, beyond description. Scripture speaks much of it, but not with a precision that we can at all comprehend. And therein lies much of the problem. We cannot comprehend it; therefore, we cannot control it. And our fearful flesh is taught by the Devil, along with the world, that that which cannot be controlled is to be feared.

It is interesting to read works of the early church fathers and study the lives of the saints of the early centuries. Contrary to our modern-day thinking, martyrdom, in fact, was such an honor that many Christians, including the well-beloved St. Francis of Assisi, sought and longed to be counted among those worthy of such a gift from God. They did not seem to fear death like we do in our times. Indeed, many saints of old appeared to long for it. They seemed to know that we were not designed for this temporal fallen life. Admittedly, their lives were not particularly comfortable. They possessed very little. Hardship was a daily matter. And these saints of old were holy beyond our present-day understanding of holiness. They had a peace far transcending their circumstances. I do believe it can be argued that in our times we are probably the most materialistic of all generations. We have reached the extreme of being able to buy comfort. The problem is that it is often superficial comfort at best. It is spurious and temporary and must be reproduced over and over and in greater amounts to achieve its supposed purpose. This would define addiction quite well. It leads us to a frenetic pace to keep ourselves comforted and satisfied. Our minds now are more disturbed and agitated than ever, while our sensual comforts are nurtured beyond what they ever have been. The result often is fear.

Please understand I am not endorsing that we return to the end of the spectrum, where extreme self-denial and asceticism are worshipped as the answer to subduing the evil passions of the flesh. Clearly, as is always the case, we seek moderation in all things. We seem to be, and always have been, a people of extremes. My point is that we have now reached an extreme of material comfort, which has brought about a fearful disposition. And the incidental fear is, again, that of loss. We fear losing the material and sensual comfort that we think we have. And the ultimate loss—in our fearful thinking— would be of our very life itself. How wrong we are about this!

I have found that many have adopted the humorous, yet profound, truth of one comedian who said something to the effect, "I don't mind dying; I just don't want to be there when it happens." This of course refers to the fear of suffering as well as the fear of the unknown. Here, too, we have come to adopt a very different concept of suffering than the early Christians had. Many seem to count it as an intolerable evil. And at the same time, Christ modeled suffering and death for us. The early Christians resigned themselves to the notion that suffering was a necessary function of the process of salvation itself. They embraced it as something that was from the hand of God and was actually an act of God's loving discipline. I believe once again that this might be the extreme end of the scale, and I don't necessarily agree with this line of Christian thought, but it did give meaning to the concept of suffering, which resulted in a certain level of peace and purpose in the midst of suffering. Some faith traditions presently teach, in accordance with centuries of Christian understanding, that we are to work to complete the suffering of Christ through our own suffering.[6] Others argue that Christ's suffering was complete and needs no further contribution on our parts.[7]

While it is not my purpose to get into theological treatises and debates on years of Christian tradition verses correct interpretation of Scripture, what I want to bring to this discussion is that suffering does have meaning and purpose and must be put in correct perspective. We must seek meaning (i.e., seek God) in all things to be free from fear. And at the same time we must realize we are not to rely on our own understanding[8] of all things but to rest in God's care and truth. There is, and will always be, much mystery in life and death. What is true regarding the saints of old, our Christian brothers and sisters of centuries past, is that they seemed to do much better with suffering and death than many of us do in our comfort-obsessed times. It is of great value to study the writings of the church fathers to understand how radically different their approach to suffering and death was from our own. In addition to the church fathers, one need only to find some good, even modern, books about the saints of times past to learn how to "suffer well." I have always taught in counseling sessions that the question at hand is not whether or not we will suffer in life (we will!) but how we do it. We will either do it poorly (through our favorite addictions; i.e., alcohol, pornography, work, food, worry, etc.), or we will learn to suffer well, as the great saints have demonstrated. In truth, admittedly, they had much less to lose than we do—or so we have come to think. I believe that the answers we must seek out involve the renewal of our minds,[9] which leads us to relinquish our right to our wills over that of God's. Jesus calls us to nothing less. "Those who cling to their lives [their wills] will lose them, but those who give them up for my sake [His will] will find them."[10] Also, we must take up our crosses and follow after Him,[11] even unto death. Now, honestly, how many of us really do this? This can only truly be accomplished if we return to the questions I posed at the beginning of this chapter: Do I believe God is really in control of everything? Do I really believe He loves me? Do I really believe that He really does not want to hurt me but to deliver me from my burdens, my fears? Again, if we do believe these things, that the Bible is true, and that God speaks the truth to us, we have absolutely nothing to fear ever again, even death and suffering itself.

There is great comfort in realizing, actually believing and clinging to, the truth that nothing is really ours. It is all God's, even our very lives, but (here's the good news) He loves us more than we can possibly ever comprehend. Through this love, Christ did the work and completely turned the fear of death to the death of fear. And this is love. And we must learn to love as Christ loved. It is only by His presence within us that we are capable of such a love—such a perfect love. In it there is no fear. There are some things, however, we must first know and embrace.

First of all, I will restate that it is vitally important to understand that suffering is unavoidable in life. By trying to outrun it, or outsmart it, or dodge it, we will only promote an environment of fear. For we will forever be running and hiding. We will be pursued by fear itself. It is exhausting, to say the least. We need to also believe that suffering is, whether we like it or not, a permitted part of life, and therefore part of God's plan (after the great fall of mankind) for our redemptive process. We may not understand this. We may curse it and call it evil, but it is—as C. S. Lewis has put it—a megaphone through which God speaks into our lives. I do not believe, mind you, that suffering was a part of creation before the fall. But most certainly, it is with us and actually does serve a purpose in God's greater plan for us—if we will merely allow it to. It can be embraced only if we are well aware of God's involvement with us during and through our trials and tribulations. God is the potter, and we are the clay.[12] How far we have strayed from such teaching.

Here, before moving on, I would like to interject a most comforting observation. It concerns the grace of God, which is a mandatory part of suffering. Many times in counseling I have been taken aback by some of the most horrible situations imaginable. I have often thought quietly to myself, *I could not bear to endure what you are going through. What can I possibly have to offer here?* And then I see, or intuit, something awesome. These people, while in great pain, have something special going on that is very hard to characterize. It can only be *grace*—the very grace of God Himself. It is somehow getting them through. And I recognize that God imbues a special grace upon His children when they need it, but not until then. We must, therefore, learn and know that the things and losses that we fear we may have to suffer in the future, we do not and will not have the grace to endure in the present. And of course we do not have the grace to even endure the thoughts of the loss, be it of health, livelihood, a child, a spouse, etc. This superabundant grace is given to God's children (us) when it is needed. This would also be strong evidence to indicate that it is useless to worry about something that is not even real, which of course goes back to the fear of the unknown. It is pointless, since we do not have the grace to endure whatever it is that we fear going through. I have observed this phenomenon of grace given countless times through counseling individuals. I have felt that I couldn't handle going through what many of them are going through, and that is because it is true. I do not have the grace today to endure a crisis that I am not in. But I praise God that they do, and that grace is given when it is needed. And once I realize this, I am free to help them with their own suffering and healing journey. There is such healing in fellowship.

Now back to my earlier point. Suffering is a part of this life, but I do not believe that anguish is. I reinforce then that suffering is not an option, but how we do it is. We will either do it well, or we will do it poorly. We must learn what healthy suffering looks like. We have good examples of both healthy and unhealthy suffering. Many of us, unfortunately, do not seem to do a very good job with it. I will stick with the term *anguish* to best describe suffering poorly. The cycle looks like this: Problem feelings (fear) are the result of problem behaviors (our addictions; i.e., alcohol, work, worry, etc.). Problem behaviors are a result of problematic thinking processes (untruths/misbeliefs/lies). And unhealthy disordered thinking leads us back to our problem feelings of fear and anxiety. It is a loop that goes round and round, and it is extremely difficult to get out of. The best place to confront this addictive fear loop is at the thought process, or, better yet, at the deeply engrained disordered belief system. Incorrect thinking seems inevitable in this world. We need to always help one another back to the truth. This is not easy in our "truth is relative" society. Fortunately, most Christians do not believe that truth is relative. Most believe that there is an absolute truth. What makes this exceedingly difficult, however, is that Christians cannot agree on what the truth is. I have heard that there are tens of thousands of registered Christian denominations. This division is tragic. No wonder we live in so much fear with such lack of security in the very body of Christ (the church) itself. Lack of security without question breeds fear. I believe our focal point must be that there is an absolute truth, and He has a name. And we must find Him.

To be set free from fear, we must be intimate with the perfect love Himself. It is the only way. We must know Him; we must love Him; and we must hear His still, small voice in an outrageously noisy, frantic, fearful world. It is our only hope. He is our only hope. There is no other. To do this, we must learn to discipline our thoughts and our actions—truly, our bodies, minds, and spirits.

We must also understand death better. We must not be afraid to die. And if we understood death better, we would *not* be afraid to die. In fact, we should long for that new birth. This is not to say that we should not cherish this life, given to us as a gift. But we must learn to know better that we were not created for this fallen world. We were created for life eternal. We were actually created for a whole different state. We are not home. We must learn to cherish this part of our lives without clinging to and worshipping it. As fearful as this thought might be, we should be ready to die at all times. I'm not talking about a morbid obsession with this, but just an anticipatory readiness, meaning our lamps are full of oil[13] and our affairs are in order. Our thoughts, minds, and eyes are on God at all times. If we are thinking correctly about this, while apprehension of anything unknown is normal, it should not produce disordered fear. One of the great teachings of the ancient faith was that one should keep one's death in the forefront of the mind at all times, to actually contemplate often one's own death. I have read about monks, of both the Eastern (Orthodox) and Western (Roman Catholic) persuasions, whose practices included constructing one's own coffins and keeping them in their own cells to help them with their contemplation of death. No doubt this sounds like very depressed and morbid thinking (and fear-promoting) to most modern Christians. Please know that I am not endorsing such practices; such out-of-balance obsession with our death can certainly become an unhealthy stronghold as well. And I do personally believe that some of the early medieval Christian practices about contemplating one's death, often along with extreme ascetic practices, swung the pendulum too far toward morbid preoccupation. But perhaps the pendulum has swung too far the other direction now, and this has created undue fear. And I repeat that the ultimate fear is that of death and dying. If we can conquer this intrinsic fear, which Christ has already done by overcoming this world through the cross, we can begin to live in this perfect love, and he in us. So let us learn to enjoy this life without fearfully loving (worshipping) it. That worship must be reserved for God alone. And yet we must experience this life, pain and all, without hating it. We must find the divine balance.

I now wish to proceed to looking closely at this healing love of our Father, His Son, and the Spirit who wants to live within each of us. For this is our hope! And this is our life! And this is the truth who sets us free!

Part Two
The Perfect Love

I came to bring you life; life abundantly.
—Jesus Christ

In the first section of this book, I described the most common forms of fear and how they manifest themselves in our lives. I also included, when appropriate, some time-tested therapeutic techniques by which we can gain some mastery over our fears. All of these procedures are very useful in helping us manage our day-to-day functioning, particularly with the more rudimentary fears with which we struggle. However, these interventions will most likely fall short of the deep and permanent healing from our fears that God desires for His children. My entire intent with part 2 is to present those thoughts and ideas that will help bring us into unity with Jesus Christ, who is the truth that sets us free, who is the perfect love that casts out all fear, who is the peace that transcends all understanding. Only intimate fellowship with God the Son Himself will release us from the bondages (all of which are fear-driven) that keep many of us in turmoil. Some of my suggestions may seem rather simplistic, and that is just the idea: we need to get back to that which is simple and quiet, for it is there that we will find the fruits of love, joy, and peace. It is in the sacred recesses of our hearts where Jesus resides, or wants to reside, for the kingdom of heaven is within.[1]

8

An Unhealthy Fear of God

To better understand the perfect love that [who] casts out fear, it is imperative that we take a look at the unhealthy fear of God, which unfortunately is all too prevalent among Christians. God *is* love. He so loved the world (that is you and me) that He gave His only begotten Son ...[1] Admittedly, in part 1, I went to great measures to illuminate our need to fear God (instead of things, perceptions, and people). But this is quite different than to be afraid of God. So many people have the wrong idea of Him. It gets back to the questions, "Do you believe that the Bible is true and that the Creator, your Father God, really does love you?" For in this there is no need to be afraid that He doesn't care about you, or worse—dislikes you. He created you. You are His beloved. Believe it! To fully embrace this one truth alone should abolish most of our fears. I think that many of us really struggle with this belief. Nevertheless, you are invited, as the prodigal son or daughter, by the Father Himself[2] to be part of His household should you choose this. No doubt there are guiding principles that must be lived out (such as loving each other), as is the case in any functional household, but they are not as harsh as you might believe. If *all* of Scripture is not read in the light of the love of God (Jesus), the point will be missed and God will be thought of in darkness, and we will be dreadfully afraid of Him. He will seem to be absolutely unapproachable. As a quick aside, how I wish we could all have spiritual guides in our lives again, like in the days of old, who could keep us on the pathway of truth concerning our heavenly pursuit.

Perhaps the biggest obstacle I encounter in counseling is incorrect perceptions of our Abba God. Too many are afraid of His wrath and are therefore attempting (and usually failing) to be legalistically obedient to His commandments, as usually defined by man. There is nothing wrong (and everything right) with wanting to be obedient to Father God; the problem lies in the motivation being disordered fear. Remember from part 1 that the two great motivators are fear and love—the first being disordered fear, the second (love) being the right kind of (reverential) fear? To be afraid of God and motivated by disordered fear, leads to dividedness. It doesn't work and does not give you peace and freedom from fear. Perfect love is unity. A correct understanding of the love of Father God is mandatory to healing from our fears. If you really struggle with the concept of a loving Father and are afraid of Him and don't believe He really loves you, or even likes you—please begin to tell yourself the truth based upon His Word: He loved you so much that He died for you. For those struggling with this foundational model of Scripture, which is the Gospel, please seek out godly counsel who can reinforce this truth to you. I am very aware, through much counseling, that being able to accept, know, and believe this truth deep in the heart is an enormous problem for many.

This primary lie—that we must earn God's love and that we must be afraid of him—is the core issue taught to us by the father of lies, the Devil himself. I conclude this short chapter by reinforcing that we must resist such nonsense and reject all notions of a hateful God. All too often we transfer our experiences with our earthly models (mostly dads, but moms as well) to our heavenly One. We must be healed of these dreadful misbeliefs. We cannot and must not base our understanding of God upon our flimsy and oftentimes pathetic perceptions of earthly circumstances. "Lean not on your own understanding," declares the Lord.[3] "My ways are higher than yours."[4]

9

Unity and Division

To better understand and know God, let's now take a deeper look into His Divine Trinitarian nature, which is God's perfect unity. This must be our model of perfection. Dividedness (and divisiveness) is the enemy of the soul. Unity is a pathway to peace. Look at the problems on the earth; our world seems hopelessly divided. Countries are violently at odds with one another, each seeking its own power and dominance, leading to wars, unrest, and chaos among God's children. Let's pare it down further to our own nation. Here again, we appear helplessly divided: there are division among the genders, political division, racial division, socioeconomic division, and religious division, to name some of the more obvious observations. Let's narrow it down further and look at Christianity. There's the Great Schism of the East and the West in 1054 (though the internal divisions predated this by centuries). The Christians couldn't agree on divine truth. Then there was the Great Protest (Protestant Reformation) in the sixteenth century, which resulted in further division. Here, truth was necessarily challenged, but then began the Protestant splintering: tens of thousands of denominations have been formed since. They (we) can't agree on what the Bible says. In fact, quite interestingly, all Christian entities/denominations/churches/ecclesial bodies—whatever one wishes to call them—claim the Bible to be the foundation of their faith, but none can agree on its correct interpretation.

Okay, let's pare it down even more and look at our own church or place of worship. If yours is like many, it has a plethora of divisive problems. We can't get along, it seems. Factions are prolific within our church bodies. Let's take a little deeper peek now into our families. As a Christian therapist, I am inundated with the divisions between members of my counselee's own families, the results sometimes being out-and-out hatred between individuals within the family unit. How about scaling it down even more to our marriages. It seems that almost everyone is aware that the divorce rate is presently over 50 percent, even amongst professing Christians. This means that more Christian marriages fail than succeed today. Why is that? Dividedness. The Enemy's counterattack against God's nature, and the call for unity among His people, should be quite obvious. Despite this understanding regarding God's will, we Christians seem not to be able to agree on how to live correctly; that is, in unity.

But now to my real point: How about the individual? If we take an honest look inside, we can't help but be appalled at how divided we are within our own selves. We often do not possess *Trinitarian integrity* (see the next chapter) or unity. How many times I have heard in the counseling room, "My head knows that to be true, but my heart does not believe it." We are in good company, however, as we seem to be the apostle Paul all over again: "Why do I do the things I don't want to do, and why don't I do the things I want to be doing?"[1] Answer: dividedness. We are often helplessly divided within ourselves. This is where it all begins. This is where the fall of man first manifested itself—in inner disorder and dividedness; we were no longer united with God, with nature, with each other, or even with our own selves. Here is our first priority in healing. There will never, ever be unity, peace, and freedom from fear if we do not begin to mend the inner brokenness and find this unity within ourselves. We have struggled, I believe, with this inner dividedness since the great fall of man as described in Genesis. But I also believe that it *is* possible to once again find integrity and unity within ourselves when we realize that the kingdom of God *is* perfect integrity and it *is* within each one of us. And we must learn to access it! We must seek this *Trinitarian* integrity.

10

Trinitarian Integrity

To better understand the concept I call *Trinitarian integrity*, please note that I am talking of the wholeness (holiness) of the blessed Trinity of God, in whose image we are made. It is perfect completion. Jesus prayed to His Father that we would become one as they are one.[1] Take heart; this is our destiny, for God will certainly answer His Son's prayer. However, we must work this out within. Work out your salvation daily, the Scriptures implore.[2] We must find the integrity and unity of our mind, heart, and soul. It is God's will. *Theosis* is a term quite familiar to Eastern Christianity. Simply put, it is the working out of our own integrity by becoming one with God—becoming more and more like him, more and more integrated as we hunger and thirst for Him and Him alone. It is in our original makeup, our spiritual DNA. We are to be one with Him. We are created for nothing less.

To further elucidate this model of Trinitarian integrity, we need not look any further than the fruits of the Spirit as delineated in the book of Galatians.[3] The fruits are the perfect manifestation of the Spirit in our lives. It is Christ within. We are now getting close to the perfect love [who] casts out fear.[4] I reemphasize, Jesus is the only perfect love there is or ever will be! Outside of Him we cannot access this (perfect love) destroyer of fear. In Him we are enveloped by *love*, His love. We are only to receive it. He offers it to us with outstretched arms (literally—on the cross). In this love is also perfect *joy*. But let's not confuse joy with happiness. Joy and happiness are not the same. Happiness is good, fine, and desirable, but it is mostly rooted in the favorable circumstances of our lives. But this is not the joy that springs forth from the Spirit, because we know that our circumstances are ever-changing and are extremely unpredictable, and they are not all happy. While happiness is desirable, it is not realistically sustainable. The joy from the Spirit is different. It is not based on "happy" circumstances. It is based in what we know. We are children of the living God and inheritors of His kingdom. We are created to be with him, now and throughout eternity. In other words, we are created for holiness (wholeness). We cannot humanly fathom what this means save through this truth being revealed to us by the Spirit. And when this happens, joy is most certainly the result, regardless of our earthly experiences. Scripture says that we are even to count our trials and tribulations as joy.[5] This is radical thinking if we attach it to the notion of happiness.

And then there is the fruit of *peace*. I believe that peace is actually the opposite of what I have called disordered fear. The two are irreconcilable. They cannot live together. Jesus said that He came to bring us peace but not as the world gives.[6] The world's ideas of peace are the same as the world's ideas of success. The world says that if we can possess things of defined value (e.g., homes, cars, degrees, awards, material wealth, spouses, children, etc.), we will live in happiness and peace. Yet Jesus speaks of a peace that is not of this world. It is a peace of heart and mind.[7] It is not at all based in worldly notions of success. Jesus is the love, and He also is the joy we want, and Jesus is certainly also the peace that we crave. Jesus, the Son of God, is the peace [who] transcends understanding.[8] Much more will be said of this, as I believe that the quest for peace is the pathway out of disordered fear, out of the wilderness and into the promised land, where we will find rest for our souls and abundance for our lives. Many of us, however, take many attractive pathways off the course, as the Israelites did on their exodus. I am so thankful that God is long-suffering with us and will continually call us back.

I consider these first fruits of the Spirit to describe perfect

Trinitarian integrity. I believe that the blessed Trinity is the profound demonstration of love, joy, and peace ... the Alpha and Omega ... the never-ending circle with no beginning and no end. God wants nothing less for us. It is Jesus' prayer that we will be one with them. And the patience, the goodness and kindness, the faithfulness, and the gentleness and self-control will certainly accompany these first three manifestations of God's Spirit within us. We must tenaciously cling to the knowledge that this Trinitarian love, joy, and peace is what we were created for; and, again, Jesus Himself is this perfect love, this perfect joy, and this perfect peace that we seek, and (the good news) He reigns deep in the hearts of those who ask for, accept, and receive His Lordship. He is the love of God for whom we hunger and thirst, and He is nearer than most of us seem to know. I would now like to examine some tangible ways in which we can strive to live the abundant life that Jesus said He came to bring us.[9] We have some very good natural examples of how to live this out.

11

Until You Become as
the Children ...

Somewhere in the recesses of your memory lies a young child. Every now and again, I have a very brief flashback into my childhood. It happens out of the blue. For me, these flashbacks seem to be brought on mostly by a smell. I long to be there, to go there, to spend time there, but I can't seem to will myself there. I have tried to rebuild environments in the hope of stimulating and replicating those childhood feelings, but success in these attempts evades me. It's hard to believe that I lived there, in those feelings, once long, long ago. I can't seem to remember anything fearful, only sheer delight. No concerns. No worries at all. I suppose that if I had been aware of such unconscious delight when I was a youngster, it would have instantly disappeared. This is hard to explain, but there was a bliss lived through the senses but also very deep within that child. As hard as I try to beckon those euphoric feelings, I cannot seem to. They still happen for brief moments in the present days—I am catapulted somewhere wonderful into my past, but then all too soon, the sensation is gone and I am back. Nevertheless, these are fabulous moments, or more accurately, seconds. I have come to believe they are flashes of heaven that I somehow experienced as a child, given to me by God in order to remind me of things once experienced, things presently unseen, but things yet to come. There is something there that I want, something that I long for—something that is otherworldly, yet something I believe I once experienced. It beckons me. And I see it in the eyes of a child. They are oblivious to it, as it should be. If they were not, they would not possess it at all. Can you, the reader, relate at all to this? I believe that such experiences, while rare, are achievable and desirable. But they happen only through a process the Eastern patristic fathers termed "unknowing." We need to unlearn and "unknow" some very bad habits of the mind picked up over the years. We can best do this, I believe, by watching and relearning what children already seem to know, yet ironically are totally unaware that they know.

In an effort now to try to simplify this idea, I believe that we can study the things around us that exemplify the love, joy, and peace that a young child experiences. I have come to realize that the children, in their most innocent form, are the greatest examples we have. They should be our role models and living examples of how to live without fear. I am aware that the world will typically drive such freedom from fear out of most of them (out of us) at a fairly early age, but up to about age five or six, what a paragon we have in them.

Children have integrity. Jesus admonished His apostles to not stop the children from coming to Him.[1] It was assumed, in Jesus' day, that children had little, if any, worth at all. Jesus then went on to teach, "Until you become as the children, you will not enter the Kingdom of Heaven."[2] Now, it is not my belief that Jesus was saying that those of us who cannot get there all go to hell, but that children "experience" the kingdom of heaven now! They enter into the kingdom now! Look at them in their innocent form. They are there. They live in the kingdom. They have no idea that they are there; they just are. You cannot even question them about their contagious love, joy, and peace. They have no such understanding. You can only observe it. And that is precisely what we must do. And then we must try to emulate the way they are. I believe that this, in fact, is what Jesus was teaching when He said, "Until you become as the children, you will not enter [experience] the Kingdom." Why do we blow through this strong teaching of the Lord when we read this verse? Why don't we take this to heart? I suppose because, paradoxically, we are not like the children. We question, we analyze, we worry, and we fear. In the children's pure state, they do not worry or fear. Admittedly, they do tend to question and even study, but so much differently than we do. When they ask questions, we adults—if we know the answer, or often even if we do not—give our response to them, and that pretty much settles the matter for the child. They believe it, no matter how absurd our answer may be. If only we, too, could really believe that what God says is true, the way the simple child believes the parent, we would then be very close to the kingdom. This is what Jesus teaches us when He wants us to be as the children. We must, therefore, relearn how to live as simply—by trust and love—as the children do. And since they cannot instruct us as to how to do it, let's study them the same way they study an ant on a log—with great fascination and intrigue.

My wife and I—through adoption—are blessed in having two young children, a boy, Luke, and his little sister, Logan. They have been great teachers of mine, and I will be forever indebted to them. Wow, do they know how to experience joy! Here are some of the things I have learned from them.

Children have incredible forgetfulness. I remember vividly a few years ago when I was furious with my son, Luke, over something he did, or more likely in his case, did not do. What he did (or didn't do) was probably very insignificant, as most things are, since I have no recollection of what it was. But what I do remember is that I really let him have it and sent him to his room for a good time-out. A few moments later, he meandered down the stairs the way that Luke does, hopped onto my lap, gave me his usual big embrace, and said, "Give me a hug, ya old goat?" Now, some might find this to be very disrespectful, but if you knew our relationship, you would know this to be extreme admiration! With some tears in my eyes and feeling pretty guilty about my overreaction toward my son, I proceeded with, "Now, did you learn anything from that, Luke?"

"Learn from what?" was his response.

"You know … what we just went through."

"What do you mean, Daddy?"

"You know, how you just got yourself in trouble," I retorted.

It went this way for a while. At the time I figured Luke's inability to remember what we had just gone through was due to his attention deficit problems. I then proceeded to ask him to forgive me for getting so upset with him, and I swear he was absolutely lost as to what I was talking about. When I was scolding my son, mind you, he was very angry with me too. I think he really despised me … for, oh … about thirty seconds. I have since come to realize that the pure child does not ruminate on the past. He or she literally forgets the past. We mature adults, on the other hand, fret over the past constantly, it seems. So this was my first real lesson in my study of children: do not spend valuable time fretting over things of the past. I want to also insert here, however, that I am not advocating not learning from the past. History does indeed repeat itself if we do not learn from it. As a therapist, I know that without question, we must very often work through issues of difficulty and trauma from our pasts. This is not what I am referring to. The spirit of Jesus' teaching, I feel, regards children's subconscious refusal to allow the things of the past to rob them of love, joy, and peace. They simply don't, naturally, do this. I think we inadvertently teach them how to cling fearfully to things and events of the past. For, we (society) unfortunately are models for them as well.

Children do not particularly fear the future. Jesus' children do not much concern themselves with tomorrow. I don't think there is much more to say here. They just do not. We are living in extremely unpredictable times right now, when no one knows for sure where everything is heading. But if we are honest, can we say it has ever really been any other way? When we ever feel overly secure in this world, rest assured, we are in illusion. But at times, I acknowledge, the insecurity of the present fearful circumstances, based upon our interpretation of them, seems so "in our faces." During the years after 2008, for instance, people were losing their jobs in numbers not seen since the Great Depression. You couldn't escape the media panic. My kids could not help but see the concern in the adults all around them. Yet they themselves were no more concerned about the present economy than were their pets. As long as they got their wrestle time with Dad and their tickle time with Mom, they were good. I'm dead serious about this. What do the children know that I do not? Would they become fearful of the future if they started to experience loss in their lives? I think at their young ages, not so much.

Here's another story about Luke: Several years ago, my sister and her family lived in a mobile home park. We always had delightful times when we visited. At that time, we lived in a fairly modest but spacious home on acreage up in the mountains. Luke wanted very much to sell our place and move to a trailer in the mobile home park. When I asked him why he wanted to do this, he said it was because he liked the way the rain sounded on the metal roof and how fun it was to be with his cousin and play in the narrow streets lined with old cars. Phenomenal! He did not value the things that the world teaches. So lesson number two is, Do not be too concerned with what might or might not happen tomorrow. If you have love, you have joy. If you have joy, you have peace. Children in their pure and unadulterated form do not at all concern themselves with the future.

Another insertion is needed, however. The apostle Paul taught that when he was a child, he thought as a child, but now that he was an adult, he put away his childish ways.[3] So, I am certainly not talking about lacking prudence regarding our futures. We must learn to be wise as a serpent yet gentle as a dove.[4] Here, I am stressing the gentleness that does not concern itself with what is not in our control.

Children believe in Mommy and Daddy. When our kids are sick, they completely believe that a kiss from Mom and Dad on whatever body part hurts will take care of them completely. I used to be concerned that they would learn that not to be true, that we could not heal their pain with a kiss. Many times, their pain did not go away with a kiss, but do you think that destroyed their faith? Not at all. They would just ask for more kisses until their ailment left. And usually it did. Oh, the faith of a child! My children helped me understand better Jesus' many teachings that our faith has healed us. My kids believe a kiss from Mom and Dad will heal them. It may take several. Sometimes it takes many days for them to get through the flu or some similar ailment, but they do get well. They have also gotten quite good at asking Daddy to get out the prayer oil (I anoint my kids with oil when they are sick) if they really feel bad. They believe, and they get well.

Even in dire matters with young children who are in terminal illnesses, their faith is astounding. I have heard of and read such accounts. Their peace absolutely transcends all understanding. We would be wise to model the children and live in that same faith, that same trusting love. They are able to live like this because they thoroughly trust that Mommy and Daddy will take care of matters. It is not my point in this book to address the terrible abuses that some children suffer under terrible parenting. My point is that children, in their innocent and simple form, naturally trust. Can we also trust that our Abba, who is the perfect parent, will take care of matters? Many of us struggle with this. But we still can retrain ourselves and can learn to live as the children, as Jesus taught, and enter the kingdom of heaven … now.

Children know how to play. Jesus' child does not need to be taught how to play. It seems inherent to every child. Remember too, for interest's sake, that we are created in God's image. Does God play? Oh yes! Just go to a zoo and see how much God plays. Look all around you, and it will not be difficult to see that God plays. (Read more about this in chapter 12, on beauty and nature.)

I remember some time ago, I was looking at pictures of starving African children in some publication. It did invoke deep sorrow and hopelessness to see this and realize these kids are no different than mine. Mine are privileged, however, and these seem not to be. They too, nevertheless, are children of God. And I then noticed something profound about the thought that they are not different than mine. The kids in this particular picture were playing in a trench that I believe held sewage. Once I got past the horror of this scene, I noticed something amazing. They looked like they were having fun. They had the same ornery amused smile on their faces while they were playing with refuse as my kids do with their new shiny toys. It was no different. The expressions were identical. The twinkle in their eyes had no cultural or economic barrier. They simply didn't seem to know that their circumstances were poor and that they should be unhappy about this. They too seemed to have love, joy, and peace. I am not at all saying this to relieve my dis-ease over the conditions they live in, in comparison with the conditions that my children and I live in. It is horribly sad, and we must continually work at alleviating the terrible disparity in our world. But I am saying that I see the same ability and inherent design to play in the underprivileged children. It is something internal. Can we not watch them, learn from them, model them, and mimic them? They're beautiful, and they play.

It is a shame that so many of us adults do not know how to play. Somehow we learned that this is irresponsible. Oh, that we would learn healthy, harmless irresponsibility again. Please hear that I am not talking about irresponsibility that leads to the harm of others. I'm talking about the need to let go of yesterday, for it is spent and we will never get it back. And I'm talking about the need to let go of tomorrow, for it has not been given to us yet. Only then can we live in the eternal now, as a child does, and then, with reckless abandon, really play hard. Let's try it until we get good at it. I believe this is pleasing to our heavenly Father. I love watching my children play fearlessly. It's absolutely unproductive, and I relish their ability to be both totally unproductive and blissfully delighted at the same time. It warms a father's heart. If this warms our hearts as fallible humans, how much more our Abba's when He sees His children at play.

Children create. I think this is closely related to play. When God created, He no doubt played. Reread the creation story in Genesis, and you will see God at play. I believe that as we were made in the image of our Creator, we must also create. This I learned from my daughter, Logan. She creates and creates and creates. And she gives all of her creations away. Give her paper, paints, pencils, objects from nature, and pieces of trash, and you will have a work of art in a matter of minutes. And oh the joy that it brings to her and her mother and me—God too, I believe.

To create is perhaps the best way to enter the kingdom of heaven and experience the eternal now. For those of you who have a natural bent toward the arts and crafts, music and poetry, etc., you know of what I speak. There is a state of being that we often reach. It has been called an *altered state of consciousness*. It is in this state that we lose ourselves in our creations. My personal favorite way to create is through woodworking. My wife has charged me—affectionately, I hope—with making her into a wood widow. When I'm woodworking, I often can totally lose track of time. I often forget to break to eat, use the restroom, or do much of anything else. I get fully immersed and enthralled in my creation. Children do this well. Of course, this needs to be tempered with responsibility to very real-life concerns such as making a living, etc. But the bigger problem, and the issue at hand, is that we got out of touch with such "reckless abandon" when we grew up and became responsible. We need to *grow down* a little here and try to go back to a state where we couldn't help but create because we were designed to do that very thing. Talent has absolutely nothing to do with the need to create, but I am aware that we tend to enjoy better those things we are good at. But that is not the point. If we work at creating, we will find the things we are good at. They can be just about anything. The only requirement is that we create something we can see or experience. This can certainly be some art or craft. But it can also be a work of music, written or played. It can be a poem or a story or a book. It can even be a model, a paint-by-number picture, or a building you have designed or even built. It can be a mathematical paradigm or a garden, and it can certainly be a good meal. These creative things will bring us closer to God, who is the perfect Creator. Therefore, we must create! We must be like him! We need to be one with him! Creating puts us in touch with creation; it helps put things into perspective; and it has the wonderful by-product of placing us in the eternal now, a type of altered state of consciousness, which cares little to nothing of the past or the future, but only of the creation at hand. Mind you, it takes effort and time to work ourselves back to this childlike beauty. Try it. Practice it. Be patient. You were designed to create. Watch a child, and you will see this in its natural, unaltered state.

Children do not hide their emotions. They know how to cry. This we know all too well. We make ourselves sick by repressing our "immature" emotions. Children have no such understanding. It embarrasses us and infuriates us that we cannot control our children better, but they are absolutely true to their feelings. If they are angry, they let you know it. If they are sad, they cry. They might scream a little; they will fuss; they will be quite noisy at inopportune times, but you will usually know what they are feeling inside because they have not yet learned how to hide it. They are transparent. They do not have a fear of people yet. They feel no shame. They haven't learned any such concept in those beautiful early years. They truly know how to let it out. In fact, they cannot possibly hold it in.

I get such a kick out of my young daughter. On more than one occasion, I have come upon Logan just heaving with tears, usually after a long day of play and creating. She is typically pretty tired. But I will come up and hold her and say, "Honey, what are you upset about?" And in her broken, gasping sobs, she says, "I have no idea." And do you know what? She is honest. She has no idea. Soon she's asleep. The next morning, she wakes, usually in good spirits, sometimes grumpy. Again, she doesn't fake anything. But what is certain is that she has forgotten totally the sobs of the night before. She naturally knows how to cleanse herself. Little girls seem to let the emotions flow more easily than do little boys. Women certainly are better at this than men. We have a need to emote. Again, it is in our nature to express ourselves as part of our health.

Crying, in particular, is so helpful in purifying our souls. It keeps us healthy. Studies have revealed that tears (as opposed to just watering eyes) contain chemicals that can build up as toxins in our systems, leading to all types of ailments. These toxins need to be purged. This is most naturally done through tears and crying. Infants seem to get this. When they are finished with their tears, they're ready to go again.

I do realize, however, that the apostle Paul admonished us to put away our childish behaviors. So I indeed teach and counsel individuals through what I call "timely tears." Ecclesiastes reminds

us that there is a season—a time—for all things.[5] There is a time
to weep. Whereas children have no need to delay their tears and
outbursts, good or not, adults sometimes do need to choose when
to "let it out." The problem is that many people, particularly men,
have learned that it is weakness to "let it out." The fear of people
reinforces that we must not "let it show." That would be appalling,
we falsely think. We must be strong, is what modern wisdom would
teach. But Jesus teaches the opposite, in that we are to model the
children if we want to experience His kingdom. Jesus on another
occasion thanked His Father for keeping wisdom from the "mature"
and learned, and placing it upon the weak and unlearned; that is,
children.[6]

On a very personal note, I remember that by the time I was five
years old, I somehow had learned that "big boys don't cry." I don't
even recall this coming from my own parents. I was a somewhat
(overly) sensitive boy. I cried so very easily. I learned to hate this
about myself. I thought it to be incredibly weak. I fought and fought
this over the years. I remember that between ages ten and sixteen,
I battled terribly to fight back tears whenever my parents lovingly
confronted me about some new concern they had with me (there
were many). My first instinct was to tear up. I hated this. I would
try to pinch my leg so hard that the pain would distract my attention
away from my emotions so I wouldn't cry and look like "a big baby."
It sort of worked. Today, though I still consider myself a sensitive
"kid," I don't cry all that much. My wife will occasionally see me
cry. And I can get pretty teary during animal movies. It usually feels
pretty good afterward. I believe that the movies provide me a safe
place to blubber (if no one else is around). Actually, I have learned
to allow the tears in front of my wife and kids. I try to find a healthy
balance here. I counsel many individuals to also seek this balance.
I believe that to cry as a child is healthy and cleanses us of toxins
that can create a sickly, oppressive environment, which in turn can
lead to fears and anxieties of all sorts. This balance is somewhere
between letting the emotions gush uncontrollably and repressing
them so deeply we make ourselves literally ill.

I believe finding a healthy middle place indicates that we are in control of our emotions and that we have some ability to choose when to release them. Sometimes we need to get away to just sob. Most of the time it will be simply to let the tears flow gently and prayerfully. My wife and my children are wonderful at this. When I first started dating my wife, I was aghast at how much she cried. *I must be a terrible boyfriend*, I thought. *I make her cry constantly.* Well, it is now quite a few years later, and she cries just as much. I have now come to learn that if Tammy does not cry fairly regularly, something may be wrong. She has truly learned to release her emotions when she needs to—without any guilt whatsoever. When my kids sometimes look at me and ask what is wrong with Momma, I lovingly say that she is leaking again, and we usually laugh a bit (her included). Not that I want to take her tears too lightly, but I understand that they are natural and that Tammy is just that comfortable with her tears. She cries, and then she feels better. Sometimes I am the problem, but mostly she just needs "to leak." It's beautiful!

I suggest that people try to get comfortable with their tears first with God. Many tell me they cannot cry. I lead them to pray for tears (in their own private places), and the tears usually come fairly quickly. I also suggest that true strength is to allow tears but to not be controlled by them. I have worked with many depressed individuals who cannot control all the tears. They weep continuously and can't seem to stop. Here we have another problem, that the emotions are in control of the person. I feel that we do need to be in control of our emotions, for one of the fruits of the Spirit is self-control.[7] Denying ourselves tears is wrong and unhealthy; we are over-controlling. But we can lack self-control if we are controlled by our tears. We get to decide when and where they take place.

Children, however, are much closer to honesty and health with their emotions than most of us, and they are wonderful role models. So, concerning the need for cleansing, healing tears—which can aid in purging us of pent-up emotions and fear—I would suggest that we do the following: (1) Get comfortable with tears before God. Pray for them if they won't come. (2) Have a person in your life you can feel safe crying with. We are not islands. We need to grieve with others. And, (3) Find an environment where you feel safe. This will usually be your home. Again, certain movies help me with this when I feel "bottled up" inside. Sometimes you have the sense that the pressure is building and you just need to "let go." Listen to this inner voice. It most likely is the Holy Spirit (God within) that prompts you to grieve. Try this. It is healthy, and I believe it is a part of Jesus' instruction about becoming as the children.

Children hear God. Some children, I believe, do this more naturally than others. But it is my belief that children have spiritual ears. They see things we do not see. They hear things we do not hear. There have been a number of movies and stories about children seeing and hearing angels and entities that are invisible to adults. I love these stories, and I too have become a believer. My belief was solidified a few years ago. Here is what happened.

We were on vacation at my sister's in Wisconsin. We were staying at a cabin next to a beautiful little lake. I was down on the dock of this lake enjoying the beautiful day when I heard my little girl, Logan, then about three and a half, just talking up a storm. She was up next to the cabin, about fifty feet away from me. She did not see me. Her head was just above the vibrant, colorful flowers that she was standing in. She was talking and talking and talking. There was no one anywhere near her. I approached her and softly called out her name, not wanting to disturb her peace, but very curious whom she was talking to. She looked up smiling at me and said, "Hi, Daddy!"

"Who were you talking to, Logan?" I responded.

"Oh, I was just talking to God."

I thought to myself how awesome that was. I asked her, "Was He talking to you, too?"

Without any hesitation she responded, "Yes."

I asked her what He was saying to her, and she said, "He was just telling me how much He loved me and how beautiful I looked in His flowers."

Now, we could just believe that she was simply saying something similar to what she had heard me say many times to her. But can we be so sure? I asked her if He was talking out loud to her, or just to her heart. She convinced me that it was audible to her. Now, I know that Logan was only three years old and that many will just smile and say, What a cute little child's story. But I believe it happened. There were other occurrences of similar "God conversations" with Logan. These have become fewer as she has been getting a little older; nevertheless, I have come to believe that God speaks to those who have ears to hear. Children can hear more readily than we adults. I feel this is the case because children are so much in the present, and that is where the kingdom of heaven within exists. I repeat, children do not fret over the past, and they do not worry about the future. They exist in the *eternal now*. We must strive to find the eternal, never-ending *now*, as the children seem to naturally know. We were created for now, this day, this moment—not for yesterday, for it is spent. And not for tomorrow, for it has not yet been given to us. It is in the now that God speaks. If we can only find that altered state of consciousness I wrote of earlier, and can place God in the center of it, we will hear Him, and we will feel and experience His perfect love. But the prerequisite remains. We must empty ourselves of yesterday and tomorrow. We unfortunately have been so conditioned by the past and the future that we miss out on the still, small voice of God, who speaks to the children because they have ears to hear.

Concerning hearing the voice of God as a child, I would suggest a wonderful little book by Brother Lawrence titled, *The Practice of the Presence of God.*[8] It is the true story about a humble monk, very childlike actually, who was the lowliest of the monks in his particular monastery. He worked in the kitchen washing dishes. Through this humble work, he learned to hear and experience God in a profound childlike way. He became deliriously happy with his mundane work because he would find himself in the eternal presence, the eternal now, of God. He, like young children, heard God speak. Soon the other scholarly monks began to seek out Brother Lawrence's wise counsel on how to "practice the presence" of the Holy One. I assert that through his humbleness, like a child who possesses nothing, Brother Lawrence learned, as an adult, to hear from God. His wonderful, simple book addresses his story. And of course there is no fear when we realize the presence of our almighty Lord, because when we do, we are in the company of the perfect love that casts out fear.

I could go on and on about the beautiful model we have in the children. It would do us all some good to slow down and watch them at play, at creation, and expressing their emotions. If we can humble ourselves as did Brother Lawrence, St. Francis, and many other great men and women of God, we too can experience the kingdom of heaven within as the young children seem to. You don't need to be parenting children to do this. They are not hard to find. They are everywhere. Go where they are, just to observe them. Children ages two to six seem to be the ones I think Jesus was speaking of. See what you can learn from them; there is much wisdom about love and fear to be found there.

12

Experiencing God through Beauty and Nature

Another way to bring us into the peace-giving comfort of almighty God, which thereby provides us a natural combatant to internal fear, is through the healing power of God's creation. Its mystical, mysterious, marvelous qualities are beyond the ability to describe well with words, since they are experiential. Next to the untainted simplicity and beauty that inhabit young children, we find nature. Indeed, as with children, we can learn much of the nature of God through His creation. Both children and nature are so *naturally* beautiful and at peace. They live out their existences as was intended.

While scrutinizing and studying nature has its place and can be spellbinding and enlightening regarding the nature of its Creator, I believe its most powerful influence over fear in our lives is felt when we simply take it in, receive it, and experience it as a gift and when we accept and appreciate it intuitively. It needs to be experienced and contemplated more so than analyzed, understood, and mastered. It is the soul-cleansing beauty of God through creation that penetrates and puts us in deep communion with His Son, *through whom all things were made.* Simply put, we can receive and experience God's beauty and presence through nature. If, however, we get too enthralled in the scientific study of it, as I have personally experienced, we are apt to miss the mystery that connects us to the sheer gifting of God through this "garden of Eden" experience. And this, after all, is what we were created for. For in the quiet garden, we walk with God himself. If we can learn to see the fingerprints of God throughout nature, we will certainly experience His presence. And this, again, is the presence of perfect love. And in order to experience this, to lie down in the green pastures and to rest beside the quiet waters to which our shepherd leads us[1]—if we are willing to follow—we must let go of our need to control and possess through ownership or even knowledge. And let it be strongly noted here that I am not speaking of pantheism, in which one makes nature out to be God, which has always been, and still is, a very popular movement. We must never confuse the creation with the Creator, for we are to adore and worship God only.

To bring this thought to a more practical application, I will only suggest that we spend as much quality time in nature as possible, and practice intuiting and receiving God's love through it. This may be taking hikes through the woods, riding bikes down quiet country roads, or strolling through parks—whatever you have access to. Even working the earth in our own gardens can help us to perceive and receive the creative presence of God in our lives. I would also add here that animals and pets should not be overlooked as a specific part of nature that can have tremendous therapeutic value in helping so much to calm fearful anxieties. If we are willing, we can learn to discern God's holy presence in all of nature. I believe that this will probably be easier for the more intuitively-natured individuals; nevertheless, I believe that *all* who are determined to practice the presence of God in their lives will be richly blessed by deliberately placing themselves frequently in and around nature. This can greatly enhance the inner journey toward the love who casts out all fear. Let it become a part of our lives. Let us truly consider the lilies ... [2] and ponder their majesty, mystique, and beauty, thereby leading us to the adoration of the artist. It will fill one's heart with love.

And if we continue to look into the matter of drawing close to God through His creation in nature a little further, we must realize that it is the magnificence that we are so drawn to because we were created for it. It is good to know that God is beauty, and in such beauty we find solace. I think we are well advised to put many beautiful things around us, because, if we can accept it, all things of natural beauty must lead us to the Creator.

It has been said that beauty is in the eye of the beholder. And I am not here to argue the point. But I would say that there is a natural type of beauty that is representative of the artist. I believe that this beauty inhabits our hearts and that we were created to behold it. In addition to God's three-dimensional art of nature, there are more beautiful effects of the Creator—things such as poetry, music, literature, and recreation are yet more expressions of the living God and need to be expressed through us. These too are manifestations of God's ceaseless, perfect love.

And let us also ponder God's greatest masterpiece: the human heart and soul. In fact, the soul is the only part of God's beautiful creation that will never fade away. And if that is the case, it should be clear that our greatest attention and investment in this life should be to that which feeds the soul. I have found nothing greater in life than to be in the company of one who passionately loves God. For by being there, I place myself in the very presence of God Himself.

Unfortunately, all things created for God's good pleasure, all things of intense beauty, have also been twisted to serve man's sinful nature by the enemy of our souls. Whenever creation—be it nature, the human body, or anything pleasing to the eye—is apprehended for profitability and human lust and greed, it has then become defiled and will lead one only to addiction, emptiness, and fear. I have seen it over and over in the counseling room. Someone has become so covetous of something of beauty and enjoyment that addiction and obsession have taken root; the Creator has then been displaced by His creation. The creation/the beauty has now become an idol, and the soul is no longer one with its Creator. Fear has now taken over. I don't believe that anyone would argue that there are the most disturbing and vile forms of music and art, and even sexuality—things that are so utterly unnatural that it actually separates us from the Creator. Indeed, this is the strategy of the enemy, to seduce us away from the perfect love, our Creator, by enticing us to worship and subdue what is, in its natural form, splendid and beautiful. This in turn imbues us with the very fear that should actually be displaced by our presence in the midst of God's beauty. But it must then lead us back to beholding and loving the Creator Himself. It is only in this divine cycle that we will be set free from fear and obsession that otherwise end up owning us.

So, finally, let us put ourselves in the midst of and dwell upon that which is beautiful in order to behold the one who made the beauty for His, and our, good pleasure. Or how Scripture puts it ... whatever is true, whatever is noble, whatever is right, whatever is pure, whatever is lovely, whatever is admirable—if anything is excellent or praiseworthy—think about such things.[3] Let us, therefore, draw nearer to God by intentionally seeking out natural beauty in this world and in each other. This will help direct us to the loving embrace of almighty God, our Lord Jesus.

13

Seeking God through Quiet and Simplicity

It cannot be overstated that we must foster a spirit of inner and outer quiet in order to hear and experience God fully. His voice is often so very still and very soft and very quiet.[1] Few would argue the idea that our world has become so loud and chaotic, that things are far from simple. Especially in our American culture, the world is frenzied, busy, and so very noisy. It is filled with every imaginable form of unhealthy distraction—mostly in the name of entertainment; and mostly all electronic now. No longer do we simply go outdoors to enjoy recreation and sport; now we can get it all through electronic simulation. Computer technology, which now seems to relentlessly run the world, can be tremendously beneficial if kept in proper perspective, but it can also superficially replace such mandatory things such as fellowship, recreation, and authentic intimacy. Indeed, technology and computer addiction have become among the most understated and prolific problems I encounter as a counselor. It is complicated.

I am always so drawn into and captivated by the quietness that Jesus showed. One of my favorite Bible stories is when Jesus was sleeping in the boat with His apostles when a terrible storm arose. The fishing boat was thrown about violently with the turbulent wind and waves ... and Jesus slept.[2] Unreal! Unbelievable! How could this be? It is peace. It cannot be understood. It can only be embraced with awe. Is it possible to ever experience such inner calm, such inner quiet, that we too can respond to life's turbulence like Christ did? In my opinion, we absolutely can. Jesus modeled it for us. The story has deep meaning and significance for our lives. We should live at such a place. We should strive to find that inner quiet which Jesus lived out. So often it seems that Jesus was trying to get away to the mountains to be with His Father in quiet. How often do we do that? I believe that this is not to be taken altogether literally, although as I have indicated in chapter 12 about the need for nature to stir our imaginations back to the Creator, I see this as figurative. We can find this place of quiet—within.

I once heard a story of a restless king who commissioned the artisans within his kingdom to create a piece of art that was to be a depiction of perfect peace. Many submitted spectacular works. The contest resulted in two finalists. One was of the most beautiful, tranquil scene imaginable: high snow-covered mountains, a mirror-calm lake, deep forest greens, and ice-blue skies. It was perfection. You get the idea. The second painting, at first glance, appeared to be the opposite, showing dark, ominous, restless skies; lots of gray, barren trees, turbulent and cold-looking. But if you took notice, in the corner of the painting, nestled in a nook of a gray-brown, windblown tree, was perched a mother bird warming, protecting, and encapsulating her young, vulnerable offspring. What a fabulous analogy of God's "mothering" aspects. The illustration of calm in spite of chaos was perhaps the same image portrayed by Jesus sleeping restfully in the boat while His apostles feared for their very lives. Needless to say, the second painting was selected to portray perfect peace.

I have always been mesmerized by the apostle Paul's assertion that he had learned the secret of being content in every circumstance, whether well fed or hungry, whether in prison or free.[3] I have discussed this concept with many of my counselees. Is this possible? Can we too find this secret? I always qualify Paul's statement with the idea that I believe that even Paul, if offered an empty plate as well as a full plate of food, would choose the full one. The reality of the situation is that often we have an empty plate—we are suffering lack of something—and that it would do our souls well to learn the secret of contentment (peace) in such circumstances, knowing that "it is well with our souls" and that in due time the plate will be full again. Yet such contentment is not grounded in future "fullness," but in an inner realization that today we can possess such fullness, despite our outer "emptiness." It is a mystery and something Paul even called a "secret." I believe it is to be found in the quietness of our hearts and souls.

Finding this peace and contentment might begin with turning off both visual and auditory noise. And here I do mean externally first. We must find quiet spaces in our lives. We must learn to not always turn on the television when we enter our home. And as unpopular as this might be, we need to learn to abstain from our computers as well. What if our technological noises were shut out for a few days? At first, as with any addiction, it would feel unbearable and the inner restlessness which lives within would start to erupt in a rather prickly and unfriendly way. But then healing would begin. Toxins would begin to seep out of us. We must learn to go through the withdrawal. And then we just might begin to hear that still, small voice within. To foster quiet in our lives is to seek the face of God Himself.

I recall speaking to a group of Christian singles once, about prayer and how important it was to get in a quiet space and place to commune with God in prayer. I was taken aback, and I still am, by how hard it is for people to find the time to do so. Many told me the only time they have is in their cars while they're going to work. I jokingly said to be sure to turn off the radio while you are talking with God. One Christian lady took exception to such a thought and felt that she was quite able to pray and have talk radio on at the same time. Maybe she could but this is just an example of our current noise-tainted world.

I believe we have an inherent need to seek deep, quiet intimate fellowship with God. This is Jesus on the mountaintop to be alone with His Father. This is we finding the quiet within, and without, to enjoy and hear God's presence in our lives. Again, the voice, the presence, is so often still and small, deep within the quiet recesses of our minds and hearts. May we spend our lives seeking out and living in, as Jesus often did, this simple and quiet place.

And to summarize the spiritual discipline of simplicity, I suggest that we recognize how convoluted and complex and chaotic life can be. We were created for a quiet and simple existence. We were created for the quietness of the garden of Eden. That desire is still deeply embedded in each one of us. It is ironic that we spend thousands of dollars and thousands of hours trying to fulfill our desire for the garden experience with the "stuff" of this world. To *simply* simplify would bring us closer to our true heart's longing for love, joy, and peace. It has been said that the first half of our lives is spent accumulating. We accumulate material stuff, degrees, money, status, prestige, careers, families, etc. And then, wham! We hit the infamous midlife crisis, which is nothing more than the realization that all we have strived for, whether gained or not, has not fulfilled our heart's desire. And then, if we are wise, the act of de-accumulation begins. And we hopefully start to learn to value those things of an eternal nature because we have come to realize, prayerfully, that the things of a temporal nature bring just that, temporary comfort. To simplify is to start seeking the garden experience—to walk humbly with our Lord[4] and take pleasure in the love, joy, and peace of the Holy Spirit.

For so many, I find that the process of simplification begins with our thoughts themselves. Start to ask yourselves, What do I need to be happy? I once read that in America, one-third of what we own is junk—no good for anyone—so throw it out. One-third of what we have has value, but not to us—we haven't touched it in years—so give it away. And only one-third of what we own we use and enjoy. Usually I will have women begin with their closets, and men, with their garages. And there, start to de-accumulate, start to simplify, start to purge, and start to make room for space in your life. This simple act will begin to manifest itself in wonderful and peaceful ways. It is a start. Also consider what to do with complicated relationships, complicated financial situations, complicated diets and exercise programs, and mostly complicated technologies running our lives … and try to simplify. I have found it exhilarating to look at simpler lifestyles such as that of the Amish, who, interestingly enough, I have heard were not affected in the slightest by the recent recession. Not that I am suggesting that we all "convert," for I do believe that there is reasonable gain to be had through the responsible use of technologies, but we have much to learn from our Amish brothers and sisters, who have endorsed, albeit to an extreme, a life of simplicity.

14

Hesychasm (Inner Calm)

esychasm is a word that has come to be associated with a form of prayer called "The Prayer of the Heart," or even more affectionately, "The Jesus Prayer." The word *hesychasm* actually comes from the Greek word for *rest,* or better yet, *inner calm,* but it is used more practically to represent the school of spirituality that derives from The Jesus Prayer—The Prayer of the Heart.

Many books and articles have been written on The Jesus Prayer, many of which I have found to be rather complicated and intimidating. This is unfortunate, as the simplicity of the prayer is its very beauty and power. I want to keep my thoughts and words about the prayer very straightforward and present it as completely accessible to all Christians, not just mystics and contemplatives (although I would argue that we are all potential contemplatives at heart). Although the prayer is mostly thought to be a product of the Eastern Orthodox tradition, the invocation of the name of Jesus, which I am mostly interested in sharing, has deep Western roots as well.[1]

I am including this chapter because I have found this simple prayer to be the most profound way to find the kingdom of heaven within. And since I have made strong arguments in favor of finding peace and freedom from fear by recognizing the presence of God within, as well as without, I must include this incredible meditative prayer of the heart as a means by which we can and will, if we practice it with discipline and perseverance, find God within, thereby displacing all disordered fear.

A fabulous little book, authored by an unknown nineteenth-century Russian peasant, titled *The Way of a Pilgrim*, has had a significant impact on many thousands of readers. I would even speculate that this simple little book has appreciably changed the spiritual life of most everyone who has ever opened it, most certainly my own. The book is about a poor wandering man who is diligently and painstakingly searching out an understanding of the challenging admonition by the apostle Paul to "pray without ceasing."[2] Under the tutelage of a "spiritual father," he comes to learn about the "Prayer of the Heart" and how to find mastery in the prayer. In a humble and gentle way, the peasant is transformed from within as he learns to pray the prayer without ceasing. Though it may seem a little sensationalized (it claims he says the prayer several thousand times a day), taken in its proper context, the simple story is one of finding God within and meditating and experiencing this presence, without ceasing.

The entire prayer, as brought forth by the desert fathers of the early Christian Eastern tradition, is simply as follows:

Lord Jesus Christ, Son of God, have mercy on me.

In later centuries, "a sinner" was added to the end. It is said that the entire Gospel message is included in this simple prayer—that in essence, it says everything that is needed. First is our acknowledgement of who Jesus is. He is our Lord; He is the Messiah, the Christ; He is the Son of God. The apostle Peter even took it further when he proclaimed to Jesus, "You are the Christ, the Son of the *Living* God."[3] Many who recite the prayer also add the edict, *the living God.* "Have mercy on me" states what we are in need of. At first this can be troublesome, and even repugnant, to many Christians. It may seem as though our Father is not so much a loving God, but more of an angry, vengeful entity who wants to squish us like a bug for our sinfulness. In looking into the matter, I discovered that the Greek words *mercy* (*eleos*) and *oil* (*elaion*) are very closely related. Mercy, therefore, can be likened to the oil of God. It is a healing, anointing, loving embrace that we should realize when we pray, "Have mercy on me." And last, to recognize ourselves as sinners is necessary for repentance and salvation. Indeed, the Gospel message is present in this simple short prayer.

I also want to remind readers that this prayer is straight out of Scripture. First there was the blind beggar, who when he learned Jesus of Nazareth was passing by, cried out, "Jesus, son of David, have mercy on me."[4] Are we not the blind beggar? We also read the story of the ten lepers who stood at a distance after Jesus entered a village, who also called out, "Jesus, Master, have mercy on us."[5] And may we also remember the Pharisee and the tax collector. The Pharisee stood by himself and prayed, "I thank You God that I am not a sinner like everyone else … I'm certainly not like that tax collector …!" But the tax collector stood at a distance with his head held low. He beat his chest in sorrow, saying, "O God, be merciful to me, a sinner." And then Jesus says, "I tell you, this sinner, not the Pharisee, returned justified before God …"[6]

The Jesus Prayer can help us to discipline our thoughts. We know that our disordered fears come from faulty thinking. We try hard to "take every thought captive unto Christ."[7] The Jesus Prayer is a beautiful and powerful way to do that. Many are baffled with just how one "takes every thought captive." The best way is with thought replacement. Since we cannot think of two things at once, The Jesus Prayer allows us not only to take thoughts to Him, but also to replace them with Him, for He is worthy of our utmost attention because He is the perfect love.

There are many variations of the prayer, and I find that each person will be led to his or her own Jesus Prayer. Though some people, deeply rooted in tradition, might vehemently disagree with the alteration of the ancient prayer, the most significant and powerful word in the prayer is the Word Himself: Jesus. The invocation of the name of Jesus holds all the power. The name causes demons to shudder. In the name alone, all knees shall bow and all tongues will confess ...[8] Although I have come to love the full expression of The Jesus Prayer, The Prayer of the Heart, "Lord Jesus Christ, Son of the living God, have mercy on me, a sinner," and I like to prayer it often, I am a strong advocate of meditating on the name alone, "Lord Jesus!" as the entire prayer. For those who are not familiar with this meditative unceasing prayer, I would like to teach it focusing on the very simple soul-healing, fear-abolishing name: Lord Jesus!

The prayer is called The Prayer of the Heart because the heart is where the kingdom within resides. The kingdom is a much deeper place—a place within where we can experience the *eternal now*. I wrote about this earlier in addressing coming to Jesus as the children do—with no worry over the past, just living in the present; and this is what I have called the *eternal now*. It is at that place that our soul is alive. It does not age as the body does. It is forever in the present, and the present never ends. We have life eternal, and we are living it now. The Prayer of the Heart is a place where we can fully apprehend this. As we pray the prayer, we transcend the limits of our minds and enter the recesses of our hearts. The prayer is not about petitions and requests; it is solely about resting in the Lord—in His presence and in His peace. It is Mary sitting at the feet of Jesus. We sit next to Mary and contemplate our Savior. Better yet, we become like Mary, attentive to Him and Him alone.[9]

In the book *Reflections on The Jesus Prayer*,[10] the author, who is identified only as "A Priest of the Byzantine Church," says there are three essential steps involved in praying The Jesus Prayer. The first step is to *relax*. The prayer in time, and with practice, will pray itself. We just need to "show up" and relax ourselves at the foot of Jesus, as Mary did. I sometimes enjoy praying meditatively, "Lord Jesus, Son of God, I behold thee," to place myself where Mary once did. Relaxing in the Lord, however, can be very difficult, as it seems we can be so tense that this will be harder than we might imagine. Nevertheless, it is the first step. Finding a very quiet place (prayer closet), where you can get still and begin to quiet your restless thoughts, will be very helpful here. And this, too, may be easier said than done.

The second step involves *finding the place of our heart*. We must learn to see into our hearts—to get out of our heads and literally picture the place of our heart. Listen for where your heart beats— from the inside. Those who are familiar with Christian meditation will not find this too difficult. Those who are not familiar with or who are skeptical of meditation will find this annoyingly difficult. Nevertheless, hesychast spirituality is "from within." "It is," as the Byzantine priest puts it, "a drawing down of the mind from the head into the heart: concentrating, focusing, listening."

It is at the third step, *getting within,* as the priest suggests, "that The Prayer of the Heart really becomes a prayer." He goes on to say that "because the hesychast is an Orthodox believer, he takes it for granted that God is within him. The Holy Trinity is within him … for these reasons, when I bring my mind down into my heart and listen, I discern not just my own heartbeat, but Christ's. It is because my body is Christ's body that I am a temple. And my heart (His heart) is the innermost sanctuary of that temple. Therefore, when my mind is in my heart … then I am truly at prayer. For prayer is nothing else than attentiveness to God's presence. God is with us."

And now back to the practicalities of the prayer. Once you are in your quiet place and have attempted to find your heart, the place where God resides, with eyes closed begin softly to say the words *Lord* and then *Jesus*. It works best to take slow, deep breaths while you are saying the name. When you breathe in, speak from your heart and with your lips, *Lord,* and as you exhale, softly utter the name *Jesus*. Keep your focus on Him. Allow worrisome, intrusive thoughts (and there will be many as you begin this practice) to drift away as a cloud passing by. Don't try to forcefully banish them. Accept them, and then let them float away as you return to the name *Lord—Jesus*. And now just continue to breathe in, *Lord,* and out, *Jesus*. Keep doing this for fifteen to twenty minutes. Since this is so unnatural for us, it will feel like about an hour at first, but stick with it. Over time you will long for your "rest time" with the Lord. If twenty minutes seems unbearable, start with five minutes, and as you get comfortable with the beautiful prayer, increase the time in five-minute increments until you get to the fifteen- to twenty-minute goal. Some devout individuals will do The Jesus Prayer for an hour or two. Again, over time you will find the prayer praying itself from the heart as you go about your day.

If you are serious about overcoming your fears and entering into the state of "God rest" and "inner calm" through this powerful, mind-cleansing simple prayer, I would suggest that you set aside two twenty-minute segments—morning and evening are best—to get alone in a quiet, slightly darkened room, where you have an environment conducive to rest and peace (hesychasm). And practice this prayer. Again, it will be very difficult for most people at first, but it will become easier with time and practice. Some say it takes years to develop this altered state of consciousness. I have found that one can begin reaping the wonderful benefits of this prayer within weeks. I have also found that many will quit this practice out of frustration. We are used to such a noisy, busy, productive Christianity that this "quietness of soul" can be very disturbing. That's all the more reason I suggest we need this type of meditation. It seems many would much rather adopt Martha's example of Christianity. God bless the Marthas of this world; you've got to love them. But then again, Jesus said that Mary chose the better.[11]

And a final word about The Jesus Prayer, The Prayer of the Heart: Over time, it does take over. You will find yourself waking in the middle of the night, and the prayer will be praying itself with each breath. You will come to associate breathing itself with the prayer. After having obtained the ability to reach that place of inner calm in those moments outside of your prayer closet, when the fearful voices of the world and the enemy and your own flesh begins to rear their ugly head, and they will, you are but one heartbeat away from the name that quiets and restores the soul back into His perfect love. Call on His name often. You will not be disappointed. Do not let discouragement get you down. It is a gentle prayer, prayed to a gentle Lord, yet it has the power to cast down all fear. If you prefer the full version—"Lord Jesus Christ, Son of God, have mercy on me"—that is wonderful; it has been recited by untold multitudes over centuries, but realize that it is the name of Jesus that is the name above all names, that heals. For those who will cite that Scripture forbids *vain, repetitious* praying,[12] I will only say that the name of Jesus, sincerely prayed from the heart, is anything but vain, and will in time greatly profit those who persistently call on and behold Him, with the peace that surpasses all understanding. Give it a try, and prepare to reap the beautiful fruit of the Holy Spirit of peaceful rest.

15

Outward Expression:
The Circle of Love

Earlier I wrote of the Trinitarian integrity, which described a circular unity of our minds and our hearts with Christ to form a perfect unification, quite contrary to the dividedness of our world, our families and marriages, and—my point—our very selves. The Trinity of God provides us with the oneness that we were created to share. The picture is one of a perfect circle that communicates no beginning and no end, a perfect balance, a perfect love. This balance, this paragon of love, is our intention and Jesus' prayer to His Father that we may become one as they are one.[1]

Thus far, I have written about the need to find the kingdom of heaven within—the truth that God resides in our very hearts, and it is there that we will find peace and freedom from fear, since clearly we will not find it outside of ourselves. And while I feel strongly that this is our greatest need, to embark on and embrace the *inner* journey of the soul, I also know that God created us for both inward and outward expression. Creation exhibits male and female, hot and cold, hard and soft. Psychological terminology has expressions such as anima and animus, introversion and extroversion, the yin and yang, etc. These are really just descriptors of nature seeking to exhibit a perfect balance. And since this is the way God has created all things, it makes perfect sense.

In order to understand better the need to receive and to give, to create the perfect circle of life, I would like to use the analogy of solar energy use. I see an uncanny similarity to the model of circular unity I have tried to describe. Simply put, as most everyone knows well, a solar panel is designed to receive the sun's energy (constantly) and then take that limitless energy and give it back through usable heat and electricity. It can only give if it has first received. And it *must* give what is received, or it serves no purpose at all and the circle is broken. The energy received from the ceaseless power of the sun is taken in and converted to usable energy. Is this not exactly what we experience as well? God first loved us so that we could be lovers of Him and others. And did not God also first comfort us so that we could be comforters as well?[2] It is the circle. It must be completed. We must first (and I emphasize *first*) be willing and intentional about receiving God's life within us—to soak it in (to use the solar analogy). But we must also pour out and give in order to complete the life circle, thereby living out the full integrity of our design. We must be mindful of the fruits of receiving the Holy Spirit in our hearts and lives. Love, joy, and peace are what we experience inwardly, and long-suffering (patience), kindness (compassion), goodness (generosity), faithfulness (trustworthiness), gentleness, and self-control are outward expressions, which will then loop us back to the inner love, joy, and peace, and we will enjoy the absence of disordered fear.[3] In the next couple of chapters, I will illustrate two powerful *outward expressions* by which we will mete out the balance needed to complete the *circle of love*.

16

Worship and Praise

We were created to worship. This is the first and best way to give and complete God's love within us. We must worship God. This is not for His need; it is for ours. I do believe, however, that God appreciates and enjoys, and is very pleased by our worship. In the early part of the book, I explained that if we do not worship and fear God as we were intended, we will worship and fear something that was never intended to be, and the object of our thoughts and intentions will own us and we will live in disordered, unhealthy fear.

If we had not been created to worship and to fear, imagine what that might look like. We would be our own gods seeking to serve only ourselves, leading to mayhem and misery, confined only to our own fleshly passions. Perhaps this is what hell is like. Does it all sound familiar? It is indeed what our Enemy, the Devil, has put in our minds. It started back with Adam and Eve. "We can have what God has: power and omniscience," the Devil still utters to us. The grand lie continues to intrigue us, and we seek to become our own gods, seeking to please only ourselves. And this does appear to be our world, and it does result in great fear, for we were not created to be our own gods. It can lead only to misery. God, in His sovereignty and love, has created us with a directional purpose to complete His Unitarian circle of life. We receive deep within ourselves his inexplicable love, so that we may freely then give it back, only to have it returned. And the cycle continues. It is beautiful.

There are many ways in which we worship and praise God. It should actually become a way of life. If we open our eyes within, we cannot help but experience God in all things without. He is in everything that is good and beautiful; praise him—with heart and lips. Get in a habit of thanking God, not so much *for* all things as many Christians teach, but *in* all things—despite the fallen painful nature in which we coexist. This takes us all back to beauty. Practice seeing beauty in all people and in all circumstances, and you will, and must, praise and worship God. Worship Him alone, and worship Him in community ... but worship Him. We are given the freedom to do this, and we must! It is for our well-being that we need to worship our heavenly Lord.

Never think that worshipping God requires great striving and effort. Since we were created for this act, it is very pleasurable, and yet we must be mindful of it. When at the conscious level we become acutely aware of our need to worship God in all things, and carry this out with simple, soft words—"Thank You, Lord. Praise You, Jesus. I love You, Holy Spirit. I delight in You, Abba."—this will then go deeper within into the subconscious level and will become as automatic as breathing. Even The Jesus Prayer, recited from the heart with the breath, is a form of worship that puts us at the throne of God. In fact, if you can be mindful about it, each breath you draw in and let out can be a form of worship.

Praise is in the heart of the beholder. Some do it with outstretched arms and contemporary choruses with lyrics directed at loving God. Others do it on their knees with head bowed, being moved by psalms and hymns that glorify God. I believe that God is pleased with any—and all—expression of praise from the heart. We introverts tend to praise in quieter and more solitary ways. My more extroverted friends love to praise in chorus with many others, exuding a deep energy from the community. All glorify God. I love to start my day with the ancient prayer titled, "The Gloria." It is actually a hymn that was composed in the second century and translated into the Latin prayer in the fourth century. It is still used in many liturgical worship services to this day. I recommend committing this one to memory. Think about these words; you may recognize them. They are based on the hymn of praise sung by the angels at Jesus' birth. Pray them from your heart, and never let them become rote.

> *Glory to God in the highest, and peace to His people*
>   *on earth.*
> *Lord God heavenly King, almighty God and Father,*
> *We worship You, we give you thanks, we praise You*
>   *for Your glory.*
> *Lord Jesus Christ, only Son of the Father, Lord God,*
>   *Lamb of God,*
> *You take away the sin of the world; have mercy on us;*
> *You are seated at the right hand of the Father; receive*
>   *our prayer.*
> *For you alone are the Holy One, you alone are the*
>   *Lord, you alone are the Most High,*
> *Jesus Christ, with the Holy Spirit, in the glory of God*
>   *the Father. Amen.*

If we get in the habit of worshipping and praising God, in and with all of our being, we simply cannot live in the irrational, untrue fear of things, people, failure, the unknown, or even death. For this kind of love for God is the perfect love, the perfect unity, which casts out all fear and is found only in Him, and nowhere else.

17

Service

I would now like to describe yet another significant and necessary way to complete the perfect circle of love (defined as the absorption of the peace, love, and joy of God and then the delight of giving it back, which completes the perfect circle). Giving it back entails the wonderful act and discipline of serving others.

It is a magnificent and marvelous thing to give of ourselves. For, to use a very old cliché, it is better to give than to receive. The paradox is that the more we give, the more we receive. It all comes back. It is in the grand design. One simple, yet seemingly insignificant, chronicle in my life is very memorable to me. I was a fairly typical self-involved teenager. Despite the very good teachings of my parents, I thought mostly of my own pleasures. While I'd like to think I was always somewhat sensitive to others, I confess that I mostly thought of myself. One day, while I was in a vocational school studying auto mechanics, an elderly woman (probably middle-aged in reality) came into the classroom. She was clearly distressed about something. Apparently, she had to be somewhere pretty quickly and she had a flat tire, so she asked if someone could please help her. It was certainly not my tendency to volunteer for such things, but somehow I ended up out in the parking lot looking at her flat tire. She didn't seem to have any idea as to what to do. I proceeded to dig out her spare tire, jack, and tire iron. It took me about fifteen minutes or so to get her tire changed. I looked up at her to witness great relief in her eyes. She smiled at me like I was an angel who had appeared out of nowhere to take care of her. She dug into her purse, pulled out a ten-dollar bill, and handed it out to me. I still can hardly believe what I did: I raised my hand—my palm pointing at her—and rejected her offer, and said it was on the house. I thought she was going to cry. She clearly did not have much money, since her car, if I remember correctly, was rather old and dilapidated. This was not my teenage nature at all, and I was always terribly hard up for cash. I don't know why I refused the offer. I remember that I always desperately needed cash for something I "couldn't live without." I did refuse it, however, and that day had a significant impact on the rest of my life.

This story may seem silly and inconsequential to some, but I walked away from that woman absolutely beaming. I felt good, really good. And I have never forgotten how it felt to have that experience—to help someone out whom I didn't have to, and to refuse compensation. It was that day that I think I first understood that it is better to give than to receive. Service is necessary in order for us to give back, or as one movie title put it, *Pay It Forward*, in order to complete the love cycle that God initiated in each of us. Here we are getting close to the perfect love that casts out fear.

There are two ways of addressing the type of service to which I am referring. The first is the most important, I believe. It is not signing up for organized church and various ministry functions, as wonderful and meaningful as that can be. It is more about looking for those spontaneous opportunities, such as that of one adolescent boy of whom I just wrote. It is the recognition that nearly every day is full of chances to serve others. This is the process of deliberately looking outside of ourselves and our own wants and needs for opportunities to joyfully tend to those of others.

The family is the perfect environment in which to start this. I strive very hard to educate my counselees that their very first ministry is to their spouses and children. I believe that God has placed us all in a position to serve, thereby loving with His perfect love those with whom we live. How often we forget this. I like to pray each morning, "God, please love my wife and children today, and use me to do it." There is nothing more glorious than to be used as a vessel unto the living God. Somehow when I recognize that it is God who loves through me, it is not at all a difficult or burdensome process. I simply just have to "show up." And, ironically, it almost always comes back to me in some way (the perfect circle). If we are first loving God, as we were created to do, it is not difficult to love others, particularly if we can perceive Christ in them. If we can grab hold of the fruits of kindness and compassion, this is not at all hard to do.

So if we can soak in the fullness of our Lord through living the quiet, reflective life I described earlier, the pouring out of His fullness—a fullness that is pressed down, shaken together, and overflowing[1]—will inevitably flow out of ourselves to others. We must only "show up" and direct it. I believe that God will specifically put people in our lives whom we can, and should, serve. We are created for this, and it will be necessary to give of ourselves in order to complete God's perfect love for us. Again, this should start with those whom God has placed closest to us. It is unfortunate that these close loved ones to whom we are given first responsibility often get the least and the worst of us. Indeed, it appears that many people are much more pleasant and servile to total strangers. But since we ideally spend most of our hours with those in our own families, and they are put under our direct care and concern, we should all pray that God opens our eyes (and hearts) to every opportunity to serve our family members as our first order of giving out the abundance that God has first given us. Unfortunately, they may not be as thankful as the strangers. Nevertheless, if we approach this service with the proper attitude, it will be a joy and fill our hearts. Serving is never to be done for recompense, but because we joyfully must complete God's love in us.

Next, I believe that we are to consider our neighbors. That would be anybody whom the Lord puts in our path. If we put on the attitude of Christ that is always asking, "How may I help you?" opportunities to help, or better stated, to love, will become evident. I am certainly not talking about becoming a doormat for others to use and abuse for their selfish gratification—for you can find many who will be glad to do this—but to open yourself up for the flow of God's love to move through you to others. Again, it feels so wonderfully warm when done with the heart and attitude of Christ—literally, Christ beatitude! While sharing a Scripture passage with our children yesterday concerning the Sermon on the Mount, my wife wisely taught our kids to just think "beautiful attitude"—beatitude. And this is what Jesus teaches us. We only need to practice the *beautiful attitude* toward all with whom we come in contact.

I would then suggest we might look for *one* formal service to engage in. There are many things that tug at our hearts, and we just cannot do them all. We are inundated with mailings from organizations needing money for very good ministries: starving children, horrible diseases, unsaved humans, homeless people, unemployed families. There are so many, many needs in this fallen world. The list goes on and on. I am overwhelmed with what little I can do. Consequently, I believe that there is perhaps always one particular population of people, or a service, that resonates with our hearts in a deep way. Often it will involve a talent or interest we may have. For example, since my avocational interest has always been building and constructing, I have a particular love for the work of Habitat for Humanity. This is just one means where I feel I can give in a special way that makes a difference in a few people's lives. I am not advocating that you do the same, but that you recognize a special interest you may have and pray about how best you might contribute through acts of service.

And one last word of caution regarding the beautiful love circle of service is that it can be overdone. We can be stretched so thin that the love circle is broken because we now have no time to receive in quiet simplicity the love that God gives to us. And, unfortunately, our families will be forsaken first. This is not the balanced life of integrity that we are called to. Nevertheless, I believe that if *all* Christians were to engage in significant service in accordance with their talents and interests—with the heart of Christ—the needs in this world would be much closer to being met. Just remember that the balance of giving *and* receiving is the key to creating the divine integrity, the divine love—the perfect love. If we were each to take an act of service upon ourselves, completing the love circle in our lives, we would live in far less fear. Those who already live according to this principle of life can attest to this.

Part Three
Thoughts and Studies

18

Philippians 4:7

I would now like to extrapolate and give some attention to one of the most commonly quoted biblical passages, Philippians 4:7, regarding dealing with fear and anxiety, which taken in context appears to be the prerequisite to fixing our minds on what is beautiful as we are instructed in Philippians 4:8.

> Do not be anxious over anything, but in everything, by prayer and petition, with thanksgiving, present your requests to God. And the peace of God, which transcends all understanding, will guard your hearts and minds in Christ Jesus.[1]

Many of us have a tendency to fearfully anticipate "catastrophes" out of life's circumstances. There seems to be an insecure part of our mind that wants to take our concerns, place a telescope in front of them to take a closer look, and then proceed to create a bigger-than-life-illusion that our quandary is insurmountable and intolerable, and to be eliminated at any cost. The result of such thinking is the absence of peace—more literally, the espousal of fear.

However, experience tells me that to paraphrase Philippians 4:7 by telling people to not have fear or anxiety over *anything* often results in glares and cynical laughter. When I am counseling individuals concerning the truth of this passage on fear, I have found it to be much more effective for us to look at the admonishment in reverse order.

First, what is it that people want in life? They tell me they want to be happy. "And what does happiness look like?" I will ask them. When all is said and done, it is peace and contentment of heart and mind that we all want, and for which we were created. So let us start there. Why do people think they don't have such peace? The answer: because of our insurmountable and painful problems (mostly of the fear of the unknown, I have come to learn). So with this, what if we were to take God's Word at face value, and be directly obedient to the admonishment in Philippians 4:7? Through prayer and petition (specific requests) *with* thanksgiving (let us not forget this part), we are to take *everything* to God. When our hearts and motives are right, and we persistently and obediently embrace this counsel, we can anticipate observing something very miraculous. Fear and anxiety begin to subside, and the love of God begins to settle deep within. Why? Because the peace of God, which is beyond human reason, displaces our fear and anxiety. It is simply impossible to be living in fear and at peace at the same time.

Being *anxious over nothing*, therefore, is the outcome of obediently and thankfully taking our petitions to God's love. Being anxious about nothing is not what we do prior to taking our prayers to God; it is an outcome of having gained the peace that transcends worldly comprehension. Additionally, receiving this peace has nothing whatsoever to do with whether or not our particular petitions have been answered in accordance with what we believe to be the best solution. Peace is what God promises in Philippians 4, not deliverance from all our woes. With this difficult bit of information, we are to lean not on our own understanding,[2] for His ways and thoughts are higher than ours.[3] Sometimes God has something else in mind. We come to learn that in the end it really doesn't matter so much if our petitions are answered the way we would like them to be, as long as the end result is peace of mind and heart (which is happiness and contentment). The apostle Paul learned the secret of being content even when he was hungry and in prison.[4] That is the real healing.

Once we begin to experience this godly peace (the perfect love), thereby displacing our fears and anxieties, it is not difficult at all to see that our problems are not why we lack peace. It is what we believe about our problems that disturbs us, as was addressed in part 1 of this book.

In summary, consider looking at Philippians 4:7 this way:

> In Christ Jesus, the peace of God, which transcends all understanding, shall be yours, if through prayer and petition you thankfully make your requests known to *Him*. By doing so in all things, you will find yourselves anxious and fearful over no thing!

19

Battling Our Biology

I would like to now take a little side step into something that is so vitally important to consider in dealing with our fears and anxieties. While delving into this immense topic I have called disordered fear, it would be remiss of me to not address the related biochemical issues surrounding anxiety that so many face today. And while I do believe that anxiety and panic disorders are often manifestations of deep fear, they are very real and can have a biological basis. Panic attacks are one of the most awful experiences that a person can encounter. There are many therapeutic interventions for dealing with these immobilizing attacks upon one's thoughts and bodies; however, I have found that with most biologically based fear and anxiety disorders, spiritual and emotional counseling— while helpful—can be inadequate without the help of medication or effective supplementation. To the chagrin of many Christians who are opposed to the use of pharmaceutical interventions in dealing with mental and emotional struggles, I do believe that all healing is from God, and there is a time and a place that medicinal intervention, in conjunction with good Christian counseling, is in order. Undeniably, I have seen miraculous recoveries for certain individuals with the responsible use of prescription medications. There have also been some wonderful breakthroughs concerning "natural" supplementation (nutriceuticals) to positively affect our biochemical imbalances.

In counseling individuals through various anxiety disorders, I try to avoid the two extremes. The first one would be to accept the fallacy that all anxiety is always a spiritual and emotional problem and must be dealt with through spiritual discipline alone. Some Christians to whom I have recommended medication for help have even gone so far as to believe that such an intervention shows a lack of faith in God and is even an instrument of the Devil. I've actually heard this, surprisingly, quite often. When I try to gently disagree with them, my words are frequently met with defensiveness. Nevertheless, I try to remain open to the many various ways in which God leads and heals. I believe that instantaneous, miraculous healing absolutely occurs for some—although I also believe many of us must go through an exodus journey as the Israelites did on their way to the Promised Land. I believe that many are healed through the counseling process. Some find healing through diet, supplementation, and exercise changes. And some find it through the help of medication. Most find healing through a combination of these. Again, I believe that all healing is from God, and we need to be open to a variety of ways in which God leads us through the wilderness of fear and anxiety into the Promised Land of love, joy, peace, and rest.

The other extreme would involve those who believe the right pill can take care of everything. In today's "microwave-thinking" society, this is a popular solution. It is difficult to watch people prematurely pull out of the counseling process once they have discovered that a certain prescribed pill can alleviate their anxiety. They either incorrectly concur that their problem is solely chemical, or they simply do not want to go through the painful process of self-examination and work through potentially fearful, unresolved issues. Much of the time, in dealing with various anxiety disorders, deep-seated fears are indeed involved that need to be addressed and healed at the core. In cases when only chemical intervention is used, the medications will act only as a Band-Aid, and full healing will not take place. It will be only a matter of time before the medication will stop working so well, and they will either continue to need more or will constantly be trying to change the medication to get the same effect that they first experienced.

As has been indicated throughout this book, I advocate a balanced, moderate approach. Not all individuals, but certainly some, can benefit from pharmaceutical (or nutriceutical) interventions, in conjunction with incorporating the many other thoughts I have presented in this book. It is not a weakness to use medicine when there is an organic reason for the anxiety or panic disorder. There is a time to realize that biochemical disorders are not shameful. A good therapist should be able to help identify how and when to treat such disorders with medication and/or supplementation, in addition to the other deeper-level interventions.

In conclusion, I felt I needed to address the biochemical matter honestly and to not let my readers mistakenly conclude that medicinal approaches to dealing with anxieties and worries are not to be considered as a healing agent through which the Lord may lead us into our individual healing. Nothing has changed with my belief that Jesus is the truth that will set us free. We just must be open to wherever He points us. And here, science just may be a friend, not a foe.

20

Overcoming the Fear of Death: The Story of Kathy

Several years ago, a woman named Kathy came into my office. She was a Christian woman who was struggling with anger and depression. She was happily married with two sons, one still in high school, the other in his early twenties. She had lots of problems with her family of origin, particularly her mother. She was also struggling with her older son, who seemed to be a bit on the rebellious side. In fact, this was the primary reason Kathy came to me—to help her resolve her issues with her older son. It is also important to know that Kathy had just come off the successful treatment for breast cancer a year or so prior to seeing me.

Kathy was very open to looking into her issues deeply. In that first session, we began developing a strong Christ-centered approach to tackling her struggles with family, particularly her son. God gave me a very special care and concern for Kathy. She was so authentic and honest, but the fear and pain in her eyes were quite apparent to me. I was a little surprised when Kathy took several weeks off from seeing me, since we had started so strongly. But after some time, she called me again to schedule another appointment. When we greeted one another, she said, "I take it you heard?" I had heard nothing. She then said, "Oh yeah, I remember you don't read the newspaper. My son was killed in a high-speed motorcycle chase with the police."

There's no need to say that the devastation of this was beyond words, as we had just begun the process of healing her relationship with this son, and we had even talked about his coming in to see me about some of his issues and reconciliation with his mom. We now began the painful journey of grieving her loss. Joyously, she and I profoundly experienced the Spirit of God in this process. Painful healing was happening within Kathy in a dramatic way. We learned wonderful things that convinced us that her son was now with the Lord. And we could begin to enjoy the awesome comfort that accompanies embracing the doctrine of "the communion of the saints" as professed in the Apostles' Creed. Kathy, as with so many Christians, didn't know about the fullness of this age-old doctrine of the Christian faith. Once she understood and accepted it, she reached a place of deep inner peace concerning her son, and thereby she also experienced deep inner resolution with him. Ironically, this was accomplished only after his death. God's limitless power over time and space is breathtaking, to say the least, and we experienced this together as we explored the mystery of "things unseen." Things had become relatively good for Kathy now, and much of the pain was gone. And then came the diagnosis. Her cancer was back.

Kathy, while finding so much freedom, had been living under a quiet fear of coming out of cancer remission. And then it happened, right in the midst of her grieving the loss of her older son. First was the cancer and treatment a couple of years earlier, then the difficulties with her oldest son, and then his death, and now the cancer was back. What are You doing, God? We searched this out together. We stood strong in our pursuit of God for faith in her healing while Kathy willingly cooperated with all medical treatment: radiation, chemotherapy-—the awful, dreadful treatments. Kathy's attitude was magnificent. I was once again seeing God's amazing grace at work in Kathy's fight for life. It was incredible and awe-inspiring to watch. Though she had many difficult times and did struggle with fear off and on, mostly she was victorious. As we went deeper and deeper into the mysteries and awesome presence of God in suffering, I began to watch fear melt away. Kathy was well aware of the work and writing I was doing on the topic of fear. Being involved with Kathy through her struggles was a precious experience. Throughout our work, I would e-mail some encouragement. But it ended that her words back to me were much more encouraging. Once when I asked Kathy to tell me about the fear and how she was dealing with it and how the "perfect love" was playing a part, she wrote me the following:

> Hi, Chris,
>
> Much food for thought yesterday [in our counseling session]. I have been thinking about what we talked about, particularly the hand of God and the face of God. How seeing the hand of God preparing us before [our son] died. How the Lord led me to you. After [our son] died, He loved us through His saints ... the body of Christ. They sent things, they cried with us, they prayed, they lifted us. The saints kept loving us. So much comfort and warm, soothing wraps. We could feel the prayers lifting us and encouraging us.
>
> Then the cancer diagnosis. The gals at radiation. They hugged me. Told me about their prayers for me. That love overwhelmed me just as the love did at the loss of [my son]. It was gentle, so very kind. You shared that your family was loving us and praying for us. More and more love!
>
> I am so thankful for [my husband and other son] and their soft tender love. It is so different, so much more than before. How I wish I could describe it. It is the Christ coming through them, in them as in others.
>
> So much—abundant blessing. I had no idea. His perfect love casts out fear.
>
> For the most part of my past I think I had been striving. Thinking I was responsible for me, my

home, my family, my relationships. I felt alone, yet I knew Jesus was there. I get confused about what might have been bringing on the fear and doubt in the past. I would like to know. Was I not doing something that I should have been? Was I not open to the Lord? Double mindedness? Bound up and listening to the enemy? Being so much in the world? Seems like there was no rest.

The fear keeps coming back, but when it does, I think of the Serenity Prayer, especially the last two paragraphs that I did not know existed ... accepting hardship as a pathway to peace; trusting that He will make all things right.

A couple of weeks later, Kathy then wrote,

Hi, Chris,

Hope you are well and enjoying the beautiful day.

I heard something today that I think applies to God's perfect love and my experience. It is that He takes the weight of the burden from us, even though He may not take the burden away. A couple of weeks before [my son] died, the pain in my sternum started. My heart ached, but each day God lifted the weight of both pains. It is difficult to explain. The pain did not go away. Both pains were still there. Seems like pain has fueled fear for me in many instances, so I am linking it here.

The Lord had placed me in sessions with you with perfect timing. Had we not already been meeting, I doubt I would have had the strength to find someone. We met on the 12th. [My son] died the 15th and we met again on the 26th.

Our Pastor called at just the right time. He and some of the elders called and came to the house. I could hardly bear to see the pain of [my husband and son]. Several of the men of our congregation ministered to [my husband] in a way I could not have imagined. [My son's] friends walked with him and they talked.

I keep hearing you say it is a partnership with us and God. Somehow in the past I thought my part was to work hard. Working, listening for God. I felt I was not working enough or doing enough of the right things. I guess I did not really yoke up with Him, as I was trying to pull more on my end. Do more, be more in my own strength as I was performing for God. I suppose this was out of fear too.

Love in Him,
Kathy

Clearly, Kathy found the perfect love of God to be manifested through all the individuals He kept sending to her and through her family's love and support. This would not seem so unusual, except that Kathy and her family were very quiet and private people. I know that the love that others showed her during her pain was not something she had ever experienced growing up. God became so real to her through these people, and her fears were greatly alleviated.

As time went on, Kathy grew weaker and was not able to come in as much through her treatment. We would do occasional phone sessions and stayed in touch somewhat through e-mail. I hadn't heard from Kathy for a while and started getting a little concerned. I then got the most wonderful phone message from her. It was from the hospital. However, it concerned me. Her message, spoken with great excitement and joy, went something like this: "Oh, Chris, I can't wait to talk to you. God is so good and has done the most incredible things. We must set up an appointment. I will be going home tomorrow, and hospice is involved. I want to tell you all about it. Life is good and full of God's perfect love all over. I must tell you more."

I cannot possibly capture the exuberance and joy and love in her voice on that message. It was incredible, but, honestly, it did not seem to match the seriousness of being in the hospital with hospice now involved. Nevertheless, her enthusiasm for something that had been going on over the past days was undeniable. I didn't hear from Kathy for a couple of days, even though I knew she was going home the next day, so I decided to give her a call to set a time for us to talk, as I couldn't wait to hear what she had to say. Two days later I got a phone message from her husband asking me to call. I figured Kathy perhaps had fallen ill again. When I called back, I learned that Kathy had gone to join the Lord and their older son. It was only a day or so after she went home from the hospital. Her husband's only response was, "I thought we would have much more time."

I miss Kathy terribly, and I do experience "the communion of saints" with her. But I can't help but feel rejuvenated every time I remember her last words to me. There was no fear in her voice whatsoever. There was only love, and she wanted to share that with me. It is not so important what she wanted to tell me, only that she was experiencing the incomprehensible love, joy, and peace of the Holy Spirit. That was her greatest pursuit, and God's perfect love took her there. His grace abounds when we need it most.

Kathy's husband was an extremely private, quiet man. He never did come in to talk to me ... until a few weeks ago. It had been a year since Kathy's passing—almost to the day. He was not doing well at all. Who would be? But he began to open up his pain to me. And yet again, the abundant grace of God entered so deeply in such a short time that his new joyful countenance was indescribable. In a few short weeks, he was living in joy and peace. Keep in mind, however, that he had lived in utter anguish the entire year prior to coming in to talk. First he reached out to me for help, as Kathy had always wanted him to do. Then he began reaching out and meeting others. He has learned of the power of accepting others' love. It was marvelous. It has absolutely nothing to do with me or anything I did. I only loved him, encouraged him, and listened to him. He has life again. In him, I have seen the exact same grace that I did in Kathy. God is beyond us. Fear not, for He has overcome the world![1]

21

Overcoming the Fear of People: The Story of William

William is a middle-aged man with whom I have been working the better part of the last decade. I've learned much about dealing with fear from him. William is developmentally disabled. He was born without ears fully developed and has an electronic device in the form of a headband that he wears that taps into his ear buds. For this reason, his speech can be very hard to understand. I think that God has given me a special grace to be able to hear him well and understand what he is saying. We have developed a deep friendship over the years.

While William probably functions at most at an early grade-school level, some of the things he says can be quite profound. We meet every other week for counseling, and I look forward to each session, as I am certain I learn more from him than he does from me. He is able to get to my office by taking a city bus and then walking the few remaining blocks. He usually gets to our waiting room two to four hours early to study and read his Bible. I am not at all certain how well he is able to read, but I have never seen an individual who loves the written Word of God like William. He totes a huge backpack full of his many different versions of the Bible, along with some other selected readings that have been given to him. Most of these are books intended for younger kids but that have good life-skills information. When we talk, we cycle back and forth from conversation similar to those I have with my seven-year-old to deep conversations about philosophy, theology, and psychology. I can't gauge when a conversation will then regress back to very elementary discourse. I always try to be very astute with this friend of mine, as I never know when he will come forth with something that I believe is from God Himself.

William has overcome much in life. We actually first met when I was a student teacher at a local junior high school. William was about thirteen then. Although I don't believe he remembered me, I certainly remembered him. He of course was a walking target for bullies, of which there seems to always be an ample supply. William was a quite sensitive boy and remains a sensitive man. You see, William is in a rather difficult place developmentally because he is bright enough to know that he is different and that he struggles with disabilities. And he is aware that people make fun of him, yet he is not completely aware of the fact that he won't be able to go to college and become a philosopher or a theologian like he would desire.

He and I have talked a lot about fear because he has seemed to overcome it so well—not that he can articulate how he has done that, but it is certain in his countenance that he has. I'm quite certain it is very much akin to my earlier description of the naïveté and innocence of a young child. He really doesn't have a deep understanding of the atrocities of this world. He only knows that God is in charge. There are several little sayings that William will repeat many times over in our sessions. Those would include "He knows"[meaning God]; "E-X-A-C-T-L-Y"; "People don't understand"; and "No matter what …" I have had William bring in his journaling, as he writes incessantly. He will write pages and pages of words over and over that seem to have no apparent meaning. He does not write in sentences, but just in single words. He loves to show me the latest of what he has been working on in the group home in which he lives. The work sheets will ask simple questions about his life—what he likes, what he doesn't, what he would change, etc. His one-word answers don't seem to relate at all, but when I ask him what he meant by the particular response he gave, the wisdom begins to flow through his slurred speech. It seems that I am the only one who gets to benefit from such discussions, and I feel so blessed.

I have pages and pages of notes from my sessions with William, but to capitalize on the things I have learned most regarding dealing with our fears, I will again cite his three redundant sayings.

1. *He knows* ... Every time a complex thought or scenario presents itself, he will simply point to one of his Bibles spread out on my coffee table, or he will point straight up and say, "He knows ..." In other words, we don't have to know. We intelligent, reasonable adults seem to need to know so much before we can be settled about matters. But William seems to know that there are so many things he does not understand that he has learned to take great solace in the simple belief that "He knows ..." He will never complete that thought, but will always leave it open-ended, as if his statement is not finished yet—on purpose. He always stops it right there and looks at me as though the thought needs to be finished. I will usually then fill in the remainder of his fragmented thought with my own searching answers, and when I hit correctly, he always nods, smiles a big affirmation at me, and slowly says, "E-X-A-C-T-L-Y." I then hastily write down what I have said, because each time I get his affirmation, it feels as though God has spoken something so obvious and simple, yet needs to be reinforced over and over. It is incredible. Most of the time, to finish one's statements is not therapeutically helpful, but in our case, it connects us both with each other and God.

After William points up and proclaims, "He knows," the kind of statements I conclude with are usually something implying, "So we don't have to understand, William, why God allowed you to have such struggles?" And I will continue, "So none of us really needs to understand why we are where we are, why we go through the things we go through, why we must suffer such senseless things ..." He follows with, "E-X-A-C-T-L-Y!"

In essence, the lesson taught over and over is that we cannot know or fathom the ways of God. We must acknowledge that there is much we just do not and cannot comprehend and that we must settle it there, as William does, on the idea that *God knows* ... and we don't need to. We just don't need to! William assumes that God is his heavenly Father, and He knows ... End of story. So we can let things go that we don't understand, things that cause us so much restlessness and fear, and just leave such things in God's capable hands. So when William struggles with wanting to have a girlfriend, but can't; or wanting to be a philosopher, a theologian, or a psychologist, but can't (although I remind him constantly that he already is, and he does not need a doctorate to prove the case); or that he still gets teased and ridiculed by adolescents, he simply tells me, "He knows ... [why]." And I then might fill in, for my own comfort, "So, William, it is not so important that we understand why these things are the way they are, but we can just leave it with God and not be afraid anymore." And, of course, his response: "E-X-A-C-T-L-Y."

2. *People don't understand.* You know, William is right. Back to the fear of people. I do believe that we were created to know and be known, but first and foremost by our heavenly Father. In Saint Francis of Assisi's famous, beautiful prayer, he prays, "O divine Master, grant that I might not so much seek to be understood as to understand ..."

At times, we will not be understood but by God alone. And that can be very lonely, to which William would attest, but that needs to be okay. We don't have to be afraid of other people's lack of understanding or opinions of us. William has had to learn this to survive. He knows that he is known by the Creator Himself, disabilities and all, and he takes refuge there—daily.

3. *No matter what* ... Again, William will state many times, "No matter what ..." and look at me assuming I know exactly what he is talking about. I have come to learn that it largely means that "No matter what happens to me, no matter what happens in this life, no matter what people will say about me, no matter what tomorrow brings, it will all be completely okay because ... *He knows* ..." and I insert, "that He loves you and me more than we can ever know, William, and that we never, ever have to worry or fear anything at all—ever again, because ... He knows?"

"E-X-A-C-T-L-Y!"

I am completely convinced that in the world to come, in the afterlife, which we never have to fear, saints of great simple wisdom and faith like William will be in charge of much. I pass on a lot of William's simple truths to many of my counselees.

22

Fear Hits Home

Whereas the loss of our home in the High Park Fire of 2012 never directly involved the fear of the loss of life, we did indeed walk through that fear a couple of years prior. In December 2009, my wife, Tammy, went in for her regular checkup with our family physician. He wanted to run a fairly routine test just to rule out a potential concern. It was just a few days later that we got the call. My wife was diagnosed with uterine cancer. It is not helpful to go into the details about this type of cancer but to say that whenever the "C" word hits the home, panic seems to be the result. It was more like the numb denial of the reality that I have seen in so many, that hit us as well. Things just went blurry and strange. The first day or so we just slugged through in a fog. My mind was a little too numb to get violently assaulted by the thought of losing my life partner with two young children. However, that did come.

The first thing we did was share this news with my parents, who were on vacation. They are the most powerful praying people we know. When they got home, the next day or two, they of course contacted us with their love, support, and prayers. I cannot tell you how powerful a boost this was to our faith. Their love and support of us began to cast out the fear. Lesson number one: Do not try to go through anything alone. You must call upon faithful, praying, believing people in your life. Get them on the inside. Share the burden. It is not necessarily good to share with lots and lots of people, but it is most definitely important to share with a significant few. We all must foster these relationships if we do not already have them.

We then began to share with more praying friends and family. Each stepped up to support us. And then we began to come together as husband and wife with God, remembering the wedding Scripture verse we chose to have recited at our wedding: a three cord strand is not easily broken ...[1] Tammy also chose a Scripture for her—for us—to meditate on. It was Romans 15:13, which reads, "May the God of hope fill you with all joy and peace as you trust in Him, so that you may overflow with hope by the power of the Holy Spirit." A dear friend of Tammy's even made her a beautiful little plaque, that read, "God of love please fill Tammy with all joy and peace as she trusts in you ..." Together, we stood on this passage and others. Another lesson about dealing with fear: stand on the power of the Word of God and meditate on it frequently.

Another thing Tammy and I did was come together daily in prayer. The surgery was scheduled for mid-January. Every night, without exception, I anointed both of us with oil, and we prayed and proclaimed aloud the Scriptures we were standing on in agreement. Additionally, we started instituting our own Holy Communion service at home. I believe firmly we can and should do this. We prayed for total healing as well as deliverance from fear, as we knew that God "does not give us a spirit of fear or timidity, but one of power, of love and of a sound mind."[2]

As we are two different people in personality, I processed our challenge in a quiet, introspective, meditative way. I took many walks through the woods by myself. I did cry a few times, but mostly by myself. Tammy, on the other hand, is a servant and a worker. She just got really busy with her life, the kids, and the many service-oriented things that she does. This is what kept her mind on healthier things.

Either way, I must say that we did indeed experience the peace that passes understanding.[3] While occasionally fear of the future gripped us both, it never hit us at the same time. When she was weak, I was stronger. When I was weak, she was the strong one. We always brought each other back to truth in God, and soon we were back in His grace. And His grace is sufficient if we can only rest in it. As I wrote earlier, super-abundant grace is given when needed. And we did experience this.

We also went for weekly prayer and anointing with my spiritual mother and father, who just happen to be my actual mother and father. It was always uplifting, as we knew we were not alone in this. Many in our church were also praying and standing with us. I was concerned whether or not I would be emotionally and spiritually available to my counselees as I was going through this. Actually, it was good for me. Another lesson: it is very difficult to get bogged down with one's own woes and concerns when you are ministering to the needs of others.

Then came the day of the surgery. The big "unknown" might soon be known. After the surgery, Tammy's mom (another servant heart like Tammy's) was going to come to be with us during her recovery, and help out with kids, meals, etc. This gave us comfort. My dad came to the hospital to be with me while I was waiting through Tammy's surgery. We were surprisingly at ease and at peace. My mom stayed home and prayed through the whole process. My dad, who at the time was on the pastoral staff at our church, anointed Tammy one more time before we were dismissed to the waiting room. My dad and I walked away while my best friend and life companion was wheeled away to the surgery room. I know many of you have experienced this. It is very, very strange, and it all seems a little surrealistic as I write this. My wife was to have a full hysterectomy. One can never know for certain the level of the cancer until after the surgery, we were told. So we had to deal with this ominous fear of the unknown. We did so with the strength of God's love, which we knew was with us.

And then the waiting began. I stuck a few books in a backpack just in case I had enough calm to read. I didn't, but my dad was able to read a little, which gave me peace. Another lesson learned: Try to put peaceful people in your life. It is contagious. It is pretty hard to get too worked up when the people around you are people of faith who exude such peace and calm.

The procedure was scheduled to take up to several hours, so I had mentally prepared myself to be waiting quite a while. Other than The Jesus Prayer, I really couldn't even pray too much through the waiting, but I knew family and friends were, and again I drew comfort from this. As an aside, I think of my little girl when I write this. I've always said to her, when I need special prayer, I need to call out the "big guns," and I will ask her for her prayers. (I am always amazed at the simple prayers of my then seven-year-old daughter. When we lived with the constant threat of wildfires up in the mountains, we kept our attention on the dryness. If many days and weeks had gone by without rain, I would tell my daughter I need to call on her and ask her to pray for rain. It seemed the skies always opened up within a few days. Oh, the prayers of the innocent!)

I was so surprised when the large, tall surgeon came out after about ninety minutes. As seems typical, he looked pretty serious. I was completely calm and at peace when he, towering over me, told me that all went well. Tammy was doing fine. Though it's all a little blurry now, he said something to the effect that the cancer had done a strange thing and had not turned outward toward other organs, but had turned in on itself and was moving inward to the center of the uterus. And while I had been praying all along that the cancer would be gone completely, what more did I need to hear? It had turned in on itself. Tammy was healed.

We learned much about the perfect love of God through this scary process ... about how we did need others, and about how we can count on His grace to get us through all things. We needn't worry excessively over anything. We are to glorify God in all things. And last, that He wants to bless us.

23

Summary

To conclude and summarize the challenging topic of overcoming fear with the perfect love of Christ, I felt a need to simplify what we really need to focus on. When I very prayerfully reflected upon a conclusion to this work, the Lord impressed upon me four very concise, and very simple, admonitions and convictions that many Christians seem to struggle with. These four points nicely summarize the bulk of this book. They are as follows.

1. *We fret and worry way too much, about most everything.* If we really think about it, it just does not make sense for the practicing Christian to be so consumed with worry. We must revisit Paul's inspired words often. Be anxious over nothing ... and the peace of God shall guard our hearts and minds in Christ Jesus.[1] Why do we not adhere to our Lord's admonition? There can be only one reason: we don't fully believe and trust Him. We must admit just how much many of us struggle with our faith in God's Word and promises. Will He actually supply all our needs—every one of them—as Scripture says?[2] As Christians we must address this faith issue. If faith is a gift from God given in measure,[3] we must boldly go to the throne of God often and ask for this gift. We must then begin to live it out and refuse the enemy of our souls a foothold.

I really felt convicted by the Spirit when praying through this first admonishment, in that worry can often be a form of idolatry and absolutely gets in the way of God's work in our lives. For we cannot serve both God and mammon.[4] I am sensitive to the idea that this way of looking at worry, since so many of us do it, feels condemning. This is not the intent, for "there is therefore no condemnation for those who are in Christ Jesus."[5] But it is, however, meant to be convicting. It should cause some righteous indignation in us to do battle against our enemy, our flesh, and the world. We shouldn't tolerate ourselves worrying so much. Should we be concerned over some matters? Yes—but this should always lead us to do something proactive about our concern, and once we have, we must take it to the Lord and leave it there for Him to work out in His sovereignty.

I believe many of us are so accustomed to worrying that it is hard to even notice when it kicks in. However, it would be to our benefit to be very aware of when the very natural thought of legitimate concern quickly moves to the spiraling result of worry. Once we see this, it becomes our new cue to cast all our cares upon Him and battle it with the love of Christ. Go to His promises, ask for faith, believe, and receive His peace. For we are told in Scripture to ask anything in Jesus' name, and it will be given to us.[6] So let us go before Him and boldly ask for His love, His grace, and an abundance of faith, and then go live it out as though we have received it. Ask, believe, and receive. And let your hearts not be troubled![7] Certainly we are all challenged with many uncertain and unpredictable trials and tribulations in this world, as Scripture promises,[8] but since our Lord alerts us to this, we need not let ourselves be troubled over such things, for we are to take courage. He has overcome the world,[9] and that which we fear is nothing less than our troublesome flesh antagonized by the enemy.

And let's never forget the power of God's love manifested through other mature believers. Fellowship and encouragement provide a very strong and successful fight against our tendency to worry. Sometimes when our faith seems weak, we can attach to the strong faith of others on our behalf. And most certainly we must also find a restful balance in solitude, quietness, and reflection upon beauty as well, as was discussed earlier.

2. *All things to the glory of God.* If we will make it our life's

pursuit to consume our every detail of life with the glory of God, we will become "Christ-centric" as opposed to "ego-centric." Scripture says that "Whether therefore you eat, or drink, or whatsoever you do, do all to the glory of God."[10] Few Christians would argue against this being central to the purpose of our existence, but few Christians, I believe, actually make this an active working goal.

Obviously, as was stated above under item number 1 regarding worry, if we are being consumed with anxiety over this or that or the next thing, we cannot be consumed with the glory of God. For we are bowing down at the altar of another idol. We simply cannot effectively glorify God in all things if we are wrapped up and controlled by worry. And since, as I addressed earlier, we are created to worship something or someone—it is impossible not to—we must fulfill our destinies by worshipping God alone.

I would like to pose a challenge for all who are interested. What if you decided to set aside one week to attempt to do all things unto the glory of God—to just focus on Him, His kingdom, and His righteousness? If this seems impossible, you are overthinking this and believing that it is not achievable to glorify God in everything you do. This would be incorrect thinking. This goal is absolutely achievable. It is not radically altering what you do day-to-day. (Or if it does, then alteration is probably quite necessary.) It is simply more about mindfulness in everything: Eating a meal. Watching a television program. Talking to one's friends or family members. Talking to strangers. Reading a book. Going shopping. Playing. Praying. Even sleeping ... You get the idea. The challenge is to be mindful of God in everything. Yes, it may prohibit some of what you might do or say or think, but that is precisely the idea. I would conjecture that within this one week, this spiritual exercise will begin to alter the way you go about doing everything—not so much changing everything you do, but your mind will necessarily be thinking of God; you will inadvertently be *praying without ceasing*, and worry and anxiety will shrink dramatically in size. You will even suffer differently, because all will be unto the glory of God. So the nature of suffering will even change when we recognize God. It will cease to be suffering; or at the least it will be radically redefined if we realize that God can be glorified in it and despite it. Most certainly I am not an advocate of needless suffering, but I am suggesting that much suffering is brought on by not glorifying God in all we do, think, and say. I challenge my readers—try it this week. It gets easier. It will help lead you to the perfect love who casts out all fear, for you cannot glorify both God and fear. You will love the one and hate the other.[11]

3. *God wants to bless you.* The third conviction I felt was that we don't fully believe that God truly wants to bless us. But He says He wants to give us His riches in glory for His name's sake.[12] We know the Scripture: What father would give his son a snake …[13] But, again, I'm not sure that we necessarily believe that God wants to treat us as a loving father would. We need to know this. We need to ask our heavenly Father for shalom in our lives. The Hebrew word *shalom* actually means not just peace, but peace, health, and prosperity. Many argue God never promises us such things, but He does. Jesus said in the book of John, "My Shalom I leave with you …"[14] And again, Jesus said, "I came to bring you life abundantly."[15] It is for us. This does not mean we won't have hardship. But we can absolutely expect peace in the midst of troubles, and we will receive His riches in glory by Christ Jesus.[16] Let Him determine what that is. He knows. Let us rest in knowing that God wants to bless us, to give us hope and a future, and not to harm us.[17]

For those of you who have children, think on this. Is there anything you would not do in order to bless your child? Anything? I love my children. I would never intentionally hurt them. I only want good for them. I wish to bless them abundantly with joy in any way I possibly can. And while I will fall short of this desire of mine, it is still my aspiration. And how much more our heavenly Father's desire is to bless His children!

I know many Christian teachings explain poverty, hardship, pain, and suffering as God's punishment, or discipline, in our lives. "God disciplines those who are His children,"[18] they say. I believe this to be badly interpreted and in direct contradiction of the Abba's perfect love. His will be done on earth as it is in heaven.[19] Can we really believe that His will in heaven is pain, suffering, and impoverishment? What father would push his child in front of a car to teach him a lesson, or deprive her of food and clothing to teach her about her sin? Ridiculous! These things are not from God. We live in a fallen world where the enemy is at work. Remember? God is about the abundant life. He wants to bless you abundantly. Believe it. It is necessary in order to be free from the bondages of disordered fear and anxiety.

4. *We are not created for this world.* And finally, without being too redundant of something I have written about earlier, God has reminded me to reinforce that we are not home yet. We are designed for another place—namely: heaven. We will, to some level, groan until we are home. It's funny how we dread and resist the end of the journey to our heavenly home. But we do. For it is related to those powerful fears of the unknown and of death. We must view ourselves as sojourners on a voyage to a great place, a place designed especially for us. We cannot fathom what is in store for us. I do believe that if we could, the fear of suffering and death would largely disintegrate. But since our heavenly Promised Land is probably unfathomable, our quest is back to keeping our eyes on God and glorifying Him in all we do, think, and say. This will bring us to the heavenly kingdom, which is within. This will most closely connect us with that special place awaiting us at the end of our earthly existence.

So the point to be reinforced here is that we must not expect to obtain a paradise on earth, "no matter what," to quote my friend William. We need to be mindful that we live in a fallen world here, and our expectations must be kept in perspective. Can we experience the peace, love, and joy of creation and beauty, and play? Absolutely. But it seems, since we were created for the garden of Eden, that we have never stopped trying to create our gardens here on earth. And, again, there is nothing wrong at all with trying to surround ourselves with these heavenly shadows, but we must remember that they are only shadows and a foretaste, and they will never provide us with what our soul longs for, which is our home, which is heaven. It is yet to come.

And a final thought I would like to leave my readers concerning living joyously and peaceably in a fear- and anxiety-motivated world can be beautifully provided through two well-known prayers. The first is appropriately called The Serenity Prayer, written by Reinhold Niebuhr. Many people know the first few lines as recited in nearly all twelve-step programs—"God grant me the serenity to accept the things I cannot change"—but few people are aware of it in its entirety, which is unfortunate since it illuminates so nicely how we are to live. It is a beautiful prayer, and I pray it often. If you are unfamiliar with it, it is easy to find online. I love the concluding lines of the prayer, which assert, "Trusting that you [God Almighty] will make all things right if I surrender to Your will, so I may be reasonably happy in this life and supremely happy with You forever in the next. Amen."

And the second prayer helps so much in putting our eyes on God in an attempt to truly live for His glory. I kneel and pray it in my counseling office each morning before my first person arrives. It is the ancient Prayer of Saint Francis of Assisi.

Lord, make me an instrument of Your peace;
Where there is hatred [and fear], let me sow love;
Where there is injury, pardon;
Where there is error, truth;
Where there is doubt, faith;
Where there is despair, hope;
Where there is darkness, light;
And where there is sadness, joy.

O Divine Master, Grant that I may not so much seek
To be consoled as to console;
To be understood as to understand;
To be loved as to love.
For it is in giving that we receive;
It is in pardoning that we are pardoned;
And it is in dying that we are born to eternal life.

Amen.

Epilogue

It has now been over a year since the High Park Fire consumed our home and possessions. Much has been learned. God does and will bring good into our lives despite the fearful losses we sometimes must endure. While it is impossible to fully know why God allowed our home to be destroyed, the outcome was surely blessed. In fact, since this particular event, our lives and well-being not only have been fully restored but have been enhanced. We decided not to rebuild up in the mountains. It will look like a moonscape for years to come. We relocated to a beautiful home in Fort Collins, an even nicer home than we had. We are close to my work and our kids' schools. Our two children were very resilient and adjusted quickly. I was able to see God's abundant blessings and saw the move as a good thing in our lives right now. The change has been harder for my wife, as she felt the deeper sense of loss to the mountain community, but she is now thriving as well. My woodworking equipment has all been replaced with newer and better versions. And while I miss the barn converted to a wood shop, we have a home with a nicely enlarged garage that works fantastically. In actuality, our circumstances are improved as a result of our loss. God is good!

I am awestruck by how much of God's goodness is manifested through other people. The church community, as well as the community at large, stepped up to help us out in a monumental way. Our particular church home in Fort Collins was there immediately with financial help, as well as meals and anything else we may have needed. Samaritan's Purse was up at the burn site in no time at all to sift through the ashes to recover whatever valuables they could. They prayed with us and celebrated my birthday, which just happened to be the day they were up there. Our incredible mountain school principal headed up recovery efforts for all the families affected by the fire. He organized an enormous community event with many thousands of dollars of donations given in the form of Christmas paraphernalia and other very fine home furnishings free for the taking. These are only a few examples of the many blessings that God bestowed on us through our brothers and sisters during our time of need. It was truly overwhelming.

But perhaps the greatest testimony I have to share concerning our fearful year of the fire was related to another event altogether. Several years ago we invested our life savings into what looked like a slam-dunk factoring program guaranteed to bring in a yield of 12 percent. However, a year or so into this, we learned that it was akin to a Ponzi scheme, and our life savings was gone. After much anguish, we were left to turn it over to God. Sometime in that process I stumbled onto a devotional teaching that said God would not only restore what we had lost; He would double the portion. Part of me said, "Yeah, right!" Another part said, "Hallelujah! I will lay this out in faith to You, God." This flesh-and-spirit battle ensued within, but I persisted in using this prayer of blessing on our lives. This story has recently ended. After all of our possessions and house had been restored with newer, better versions (with a substantially lower mortgage payment), we got our final insurance check in the mail two weeks ago. It was above and beyond everything else, as all had already been paid for by insurance proceeds. The amount of our final insurance check was for exactly twice what we lost in the Ponzi scheme. Praise be to our Lord and God for His goodness! We need not fear.

And as I write these final words about the perfect love of God, which casts out all our fears, I am dreadfully sensitive to those who have stood before the Lord with their greatest fears as Tammy and I did with her cancer and the loss of our home, only to have those fears realized. Kathy (see chapter 20) didn't survive her cancer, and

I have been privileged to help her grieving husband through this mystery as to why some are healed and some are not. God's grace has become abundant in his life, as it had in Kathy's; none of us can claim to understand the enigma of life and death through the eyes of Abba God. The older I get, the larger my "I don't know" category seems to become. And as strange as it may seem, I can take comfort in knowing that as I rest in God's sovereignty in all things, all things will work together for good.[1] If we believe that God is in control of all things, and that He loves us (as the Holy Scriptures profess), then we need not ever fear incorrectly again, because, while we may never know ... He knows ... (Thank you, William! See chapter 21). Let not your hearts be troubled.[2] Blessed be His name!

> So, fear not ... for He [God] Himself has said, I will not in any way fail you nor give you up nor leave you without support. [I will] not, [I will] not, [I will] not in any degree leave you helpless nor forsake nor let [you] down [relax my hold on you]! [Assuredly not!] So we take comfort and are encouraged and confidently and boldly say, The Lord is my helper; I will not be seized with alarm [I will not fear or dread or be terrified]. What can man do to me? (Hebrews 13:5–6, Amplified Version).

Amen and amen!

Notes

Part One: Understanding Fear

Chapter 1: Fear: The Great Paradox
[1] M. Scott Peck, *The Road Less Traveled* (New York: Touchstone: Simon and Schuster, 1978).
[2] Matthew 6:24
[3] Matthew 6:21
[4] Matthew 6:20
[5] John 10:10
[6] John 14:27

Chapter 2: The Five Fears
[1] Genesis 1: 10, 25, 31

Chapter 3: First-Level Fear: The Fear of Things
[1] Timothy 1:7
[2] Galatians 6:2
[3] John 8:32
[4] 2 Corinthians 10:5
[5] Romans 12:2
[6] Proverbs 23:7
[7] 1 John 4:18

Chapter 4: Second-Level Fear: The Fear of People
[1] Matthew 19:19; Luke 10:27; Romans 13:9; Galatians 5:14; James 2:8
[2] Ephesians 4:26
[3] 1 John 4:18

[4] Hebrews 12:15
[5] John 8:32
[6] Colossians 1:17

Chapter 5: Third-Level Fear: The Fear of Failure

[1] Psalm 23:1
[2] Matthew 11:28–30

Chapter 6: Fourth-Level Fear: The Fear of the Unknown/ The Fear of Loss

[3] Corinthians 12:4–11
[4] Psalm 46:10

Chapter 7: Fifth-Level Fear: The Fear of Suffering and Death

[1] Hebrews 2:15
[2] 1 Corinthians 2:9
[3] Philippians 1:21
[4] Revelation 7:17; 21:4
[5] 2 Corinthians 5:1–5
[6] Colossians 1:24
[7] Hebrews 5:9
[8] Proverbs 3:5
[9] Romans 12:2
[10] Matthew 10:39
[11] Matthew 16:24; Mark 8:34; Luke 9:23
[12] Isaiah 64:8
[13] Matthew 25:3–4

Part Two: The Perfect Love

[1] Luke 17:21

Chapter 8: An Unhealthy Fear of God

[1] John 3:16
[2] Luke 15:11–32
[3] Proverbs 3:5
[4] Isaiah 55:9

Chapter 9: Unity and Division
[1] Romans 7:15

Chapter 10: Trinitarian Integrity
[1] John 17:11, 21–22
[2] Philippians 2:12
[3] Galatians 5:22–23
[4] 1 John 4:18
[5] James 1:2
[6] John 14:27
[7] Philippians 4:7
[8] Philippians 4:7
[9] John 10:10

Chapter 11: Until You Become As the Children ...
[1] Matthew 19:14
[2] Matthew 18:3
[3] 1 Corinthians 13:11
[4] Matthew 10:16
[5] Ecclesiastes 3:1
[6] Luke 10:21
[7] Galatians 5:23
[8] Brother Lawrence, *The Practice of the Presence of God & The Spiritual Maxims* (Benton Press: 2013).

Chapter 12: Experiencing God through Beauty and Nature
[1] Psalm 23:2
[2] Matthew 6:28–29
[3] Philippians 4:8

Chapter 13: Seeking God through Quiet and Simplicity
[1] Kings 19:12
[2] Luke 8:22–25
[3] Philippians 4:12
[4] Micah 6:8

Chapter 14: Hesychasm (Inner Calm)

1. Rama Coomaraswamy, *The Invocation of the Name of Jesus* (Louisville, Kentucky: Fons Vitae, 1999).
2. 1 Thessalonians 5:17
3. Matthew 16:16
4. Luke 18:35–38
5. Luke 17:12–13
6. Luke 18:9–14
7. 2 Corinthians 10:5
8. Romans 14:11
9. Luke 10:39
10. A Priest of the Byzantine Church (anonymous), *Reflections on The Jesus Prayer* (Denville, New Jersey: Dimension Books, 1978).
11. Luke 10:41–42
12. Matthew 6:7

Chapter 15: Outward Expression: The Circle of Love

1. John 17:11, 21–22
2. 2 Corinthians 1:4
3. Galatians 5:22–23

Chapter 16: Worship and Praise

Chapter 17: Service

1. Luke 6:38

Part Three

Chapter 18: Philippians 4:7

1. Philippians 4:7
2. Proverbs 3:5
3. Isaiah 55:9
4. Philippians 4:11

Chapter 19: Battling Our Biology

Chapter 20: Overcoming the Fear of Death: The Story of Kathy

1. John 16:33

Chapter 21: Overcoming the Fear of People: The Story of William

Chapter 22: Fear Hits Home
[1] Ecclesiastes 4:12
[2] 2 Timothy 1:7
[3] Philippians 4:7

Summary
[1] Philippians 4:6
[2] Philippians 4:19
[3] Romans 12:3
[4] Matthew 6:24
[5] Romans 8:1
[6] John 14:13; 16:24
[7] John 14:27
[8] John 16:33
[9] John 16:33
[10] 1 Corinthians 10:31
[11] Matthew 6:24
[12] Philippians 4:19
[13] Matthew 9:10–11
[14] John 14:27
[15] John 10:10
[16] Philippians 4:19
[17] Jeremiah 29:11
[18] Hebrews 12:7
[19] Matthew 6:10

Epilogue
[1] Romans 8:28
[2] John 14:27

CPSIA information can be obtained at www.ICGtesting.com
Printed in the USA
LVOW11s2053110214

373243LV00002B/4/P